FOLLOWING JESUS
ALL THE WAY

ELLY

December 1987

Dear Bro + Si Sinion.

*May the Lord bless you as
you serve as Teacher +
Missions Sec —*

Merry Christmas

The Sun Sch Dept

*FOLLOWING JESUS
ALL THE WAY*

Elly Hansen and Mary Wallace

Elly

by Elly Hansen and Mary Wallace

©1987 Word Aflame Press
Hazelwood, MO 63042-2299

Cover Design by Tim Angew

Printed in United States of America.

Printed by

Library of Congress Cataloging-in-Publication Data

Hansey, Elly, 1921-
    Elly: followed Jesus all the way.

    1. Hansen, Elly, 1921-   .   2. Missionaries—Thailand—Biography.
3. Missionaries—Denmark—Biography. I. Wallace, Mary H. II. Title.
BV3317.H36A3 1988   266'.0092'4 [B]   87-23094
ISBN 0-932581-23-4

Contents

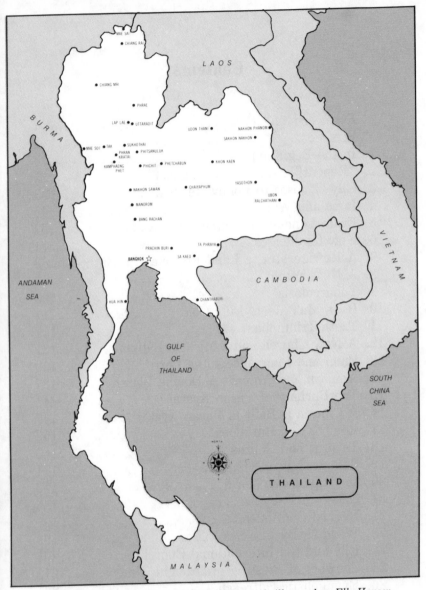

Map of Thailand showing some of the towns and villages where Elly Hansen and the Pentecostals of Thailand minister.

Foreword

What a challenging message we often receive through a well-told story. This is a remarkable story of a remarkable life.

Mary Wallace has for several years felt a burden and had a vision to present on-coming generations with the life stories of our early heroes of the faith. She has enriched our lives by recording the stories of many outstanding people, including many ministers and missionaries.

Sister Elly Hansen is one of those unusual and outstanding people. When Brother and Sister Billy Cole arrived in Thailand with their daughter, Brenda, Sister Elly belonged to the World Evangelism Crusade. She felt that the Coles were in heresy and that they had come to Thailand to spread their false teachings, so she called her group together and told them, "If we pray very diligently, perhaps they will not get a visa." But after a while the visa came through. Then she went back to her group. "If we pray very hard, perhaps they will not learn the language." Brother Cole said they thought for some time that perhaps the Lord was answering her prayer. After months of effort and struggle, they learned the Thai language.

Even though Sister Elly was praying that the Coles would not be able to stay in Thailand, she kept returning to the conferences and camp meetings. She could not seem to stay away. Eventually God got hold of her heart, and she came forward to be baptized in Jesus' name along with others. God had His hand on this beautiful handmaiden as He had already filled her with the Holy Spirit and placed such a hunger in her heart for more of God.

Sister Wallace takes us back to Elly's early childhood in Denmark, through the estrangement from her father, her determination to equip herself for her call, and her exciting and fulfilling life as a missionary in Thailand.

You will be thrilled and challenged as you read what God can do with a heart that hungers after Him. Elly desires that God alone will receive glory through the story of her life, a life lived for God alone, glorifying Him and challenging us.

Audrene Seism

Preface

In 1975 the Bectons and the Wallaces made a trip to Thailand on behalf of the Sunday School Division of the United Pentecostal Church International. In Bangkok I met Elly Hansen for the first time, and she invited us to Phran Kratai if we ever came again. The next year my husband and I toured Asia again with the Fred Kinzies, and this time we drove all day from Bangkok to Phran Kratai. On the return trip Ping drove Sister Elly and me in the Toyota pickup, and I had several hours to talk just with her. By this time I realized that I was meeting a most significant person. As I questioned her about her background, she shared story after story full of action, color, and drama that clearly portrayed the hand of God upon a committed person. "You need to write a book, Sister Elly," I urged, but Elly Hansen was far too busy living a story to take time to put it on paper. She even dreaded writing a newsletter, although her letters are interesting and full of word pictures.

She mentioned her upcoming furlough, and I insisted that she plan to stay with us when she was at headquarters. When she arrived I had a hard time keeping up with her active schedule, but I insisted that we take some time to tape interviews. Sister Elly is a tremendous storyteller and a great communicator. The interviews filled nine tapes!

Marie Yarbrough was my secretary at the time, and she began transcribing the tapes immediately so that Sister Hansen could look them over before we left for the world conference in Jerusalem.

After the conference I became involved in compiling and writing other books, so I put my notes on the Elly Hansen story away, thinking I would try to have the book ready when she returned in four years on another furlough.

Time passed, and when I inquired, I was told that she would not leave Thailand on furlough because of a visa difficulty. In 1985 I thought surely she would attend the world conference in Manila but again she did not want to risk losing her visa and so chose to remain at her post in Phran Kratai. When I first heard of her problem with cancer, I immediately got my notes out and began to refresh my memory because I knew I had a wonderful story to share.

Brother Harry Scism, director of foreign missions, contacted my husband and me about taking a trip to Bangkok to gather more material, especially on the story since 1980. When I arrived in Bangkok I realized that we were just in time. Although Sister Hansen was in much pain and very weak, she was lucid, cooperative, and glad to share all she could. She insisted, however, that she wanted no glory. "God must get all the glory! He is everything; I am nothing," she repeated.

Because of the radiation being given directly on the throat area, it was difficult for Sister Hansen to talk at length, but she gladly answered questions that I had organized, and she occasionally embellished an incident with an amusing comment.

The story that I have written is based on her recollection of events. Since she is Danish, her spelling does not always coincide with American spelling, and I have tried to make the spelling of names and places uniform. Regarding the names of places in Thailand, Brother Chaiyong bought me a government map and suggested that we use its spelling, although it differs from the spelling Sister Elly has used in her newsletters. She agreed with that decision, so Prankadai becomes Phran Kratai and Jenberry near the Cambodian border, becomes Chantaburi.

Brother Chaiyong read part of the manuscript, and he was most helpful in many ways, particularly in driving us back and forth from the YMCA where we stayed to the hospital. It is obvious that he and his wife have worked closely with Sister Hansen to spread the Pentecostal message in Thailand. Of course, both of them give credit to Brother and Sister Billy Cole for their great work of bringing the full truth of the Oneness of God and Jesus Name baptism to Thailand and continuing year after year to tour, travel, preach, and teach.

Many others have contributed ideas and information, including the C. M. Bectons, the Harry Scisms, the Jack Leamans, F. B. Poling, the Marvin Coles, Robert Mitchell, Paul Cook, the Everett Corcorans, Margie Kuhn, and Mary Loudermilk. I gratefully thank all of them as well as my secretary, Margie McNall, and my co-worker, Georgia Smelser, for listening and providing ideas and Edna Nation, who encouraged me concerning the last chapter.

For information regarding the nation of Denmark, the staff member at the Danish Embassy in Washington was very helpful, sending me quite a bit of reading material as well as giving me the name of the Nordic Press, where more material was available. The Embassy of Thailand also responded with maps, brochures, and materials.

My thanks also goes to my very best friend and staunchest supporter, my husband, without whose help, prodding, and encouragement I would probably not do too much of anything, because I am basically a very lazy person and writing is very hard work. But he constantly challenges me in every area of my life to do my very best.

Concerning this book, however, my deepest appreciation goes to Elly Hansen who has lived such a challenging, committed Christian life that I felt I simply must get it on paper as best I could to share it with everyone. May God bless all who read this story, and may this book challenge the reader to follow Him all the way.

Mary H. Wallace

Chapter 1
. . . .

In the Beginning

"If you want to follow Jesus, well, follow Him. But not here!" Christian Anders Hansen slammed his fist on the kitchen table and yelled at his seventeen-year-old daughter, Elly. "If you want a home with me, you cannot follow Jesus. Take your religion and get out. I need a good barmaid, not a religious fanatic. Now make up your mind what you are going to do. Follow Jesus? Then pack your stuff and follow Him. See where He will lead you." The tall, hostile, irate, red-faced Dane glared at his oldest child.

"I will follow Jesus," Elly decided.

"Well, you have had your last meal here then," Christian shouted harshly. "Go ahead! Follow Jesus and see what happens to you!"

Elly had a deep hunger that her father's food did not satisfy. Trembling and anxious, but just as determined as her father, young Elly Hansen made an expensive decision. She packed her suitcase and left her father's home in Frederiksvaerk, Denmark. She was not to return for thirteen years.

* * * * * * * *

Denmark, the home of the Hansen family, is made up of the peninsula of Jutland, which is an extension of the continent of Europe, and five hundred islands, of which one hundred are inhabited. The Hansens lived on Zealand, the island on which Copenhagen, the capital, is situated. From one end of Denmark to the other, no Dane lives more than thirty miles or so from the coast. The nation is mostly lowland, with the highest hill being only a little more than five hundred feet.

Elly's father, Christian Anders Hansen, had been reared by a stern, strict, well-educated father. Valdemar Hansen had a job with the police, and he saw to it that his son, Christian, had a proper education. The Hansen's home town was the coastal harbor town of Frederiksvaerk in the north of Zealand. Although not quite as tall as his father, who measured six feet four inches, Christian stood over six feet tall.

As a young man, Christian Anders Hansen became a soldier in the Life Guard of King Christian. He was stationed at Rungsted, an ancient town that dated back to A.D. 1100. Here the twenty-two-year-old soldier met and married a small, quiet, blue-eyed girl, Elna Margrete Mogensen.

Perhaps Christian's military background contributed to his harsh, inflexible attitude toward his daughter. Christian felt proud of his army experience. "One of my soldier friends was the father of the queen of Denmark," he was fond of declaring.

On Monday, July 5, 1921, a blue-eyed, bald-headed baby girl, Elly, was born to this young soldier and his bride.

"A girl! I thought I would father a boy," Christian groused. "Well, she has no hair, but she looks strong and well. I will train her in gymnastics even if she is a girl!"

Elna, a submissive wife, held the baby girl tightly and suggested timidly, "Let's call her Elly—just Elly, no middle name. She looks just like your mother, Christian. I will make her some pretty little bonnets until her hair grows out." Elna made bonnets for Elly until she was four years old.

Also in July 1921, to the south of Denmark in Germany, a frustrated artist who sometimes worked as a paperhanger became the undisputed leader of the Nazi political party. At that time Hitler was no more than a "cloud the size of a man's hand," but he soon began to stir up storm that would engulf all of Europe, including Denmark, and would change the world in which Elly grew up.

When Elly Hansen was three months old, Christian and Elna carried their daughter to the Lutheran church to be sprinkled. Elna had carefully made the baby's christening outfit, complete with a beautiful bonnet that concealed the baby's lack of hair. But Christian had no respect at all for God or the church and very little interest in Elly's infant baptism.

"They're just a bunch of hypocrites," he declared. "We don't need to go to church!"

During the Middle Ages, Christianity had come to Denmark in the form of the Catholic church, but the

Lutheran church has been the state church since the sixteenth century.

The reformer of the Danish church was a monk, Hans Taven, who after a visit to Luther in Wittenberg, began preaching the new ideas of Protestantism in Copenhagen. He received the protection of King Frederik I despite that in his coronation charter the king had promised to uphold the Roman Catholic Church. The king's oldest son, Christian, had personally attended Luther's plea at Worms in 1521 and had become a convinced and declared Lutheran.

In 1533 when Frederik I died, the Catholic bishops and the majority of the aristocrats refused to elect Christian as successor because of his Lutheran convictions. A civil war broke out between the Catholic aristocrats and the peasants. On July 4, 1534, Mogens Goye, the leader of the Lutheran minority of the aristocrats, convinced the other lords to elect Frederik I's eldest son as King Christian III. The oldest of the bishops burst out weeping. He knew that this meant the end of the Catholic church in Denmark. The Catholic church, possessing one-third of all land in Denmark, was then forced to pay for the war.

King Christian III was now the head of the state church, the Lutheran church. All tithes went to the state, and the church ministers became civil servants. Christian III asked a Danish author, Christian Pedersen, to translate the entire Bible into Danish, and his translation was printed in 1550. Pedersen became "the father of written Danish," as his Bible became the standard reference for future authors.

Only Lutheran churches were allowed in Denmark, and a committee of three professors of theology censored everything that was printed.

Today ninety-eight percent of all Danes belong to the Lutheran state church. When a baby is born in Denmark, he is registered in a church book within forty-eight hours after birth. Thus Danes believe that they are Christians from birth because they are born into a "Christian" nation.

After Elly was born Christian left the army, and the family moved to his home town, Frederiksvaerk, on the northern coast of Zealand. There he bought a hotel and settled down to his own business, still indifferent and almost hostile to God and the church as well as to so-called Christians.

Although Christian wanted a boy badly, Elly began early to show her father that she would become a strong, courageous, determined person much like his mother. A cute, curly-haired strawberry blonde, Elly enjoyed music. She began dancing when she was three years old. Later she learned ballet, folk dancing, and ballroom dancing, and her father began to use her to dance for the hotel guests. Her grandmother taught her to knit and crochet. Always active and outgoing, Elly enjoyed her little world, which consisted of her quiet, submissive, devoted mother and her aggressive, successful businessman father as well as the constant flow of guests in the hotel.

Elly's childhood contained dilemmas as well as delights, sorrows as well as joys. One Easter Elna made Elly a pretty little apricot dress with matching panties. Easter in Denmark means many colored boiled eggs. So Elly joined the family next door, and they rolled eggs down the hill. Instead of walking down hill to collect her eggs, Elly scooted down. "Oh, Elly, you have ruined your beautiful Easter outfit." Punishment followed swiftly.

That summer Elly learned a few more lessons concerning things she could not do.

One day she climbed upon a fence covered with beautiful, fragrant sweet peas to ponder life. As she sat there in her imagination Elly saw a little airplane with just two people in it. She heard a voice say, "Really, you are a lucky little girl, and a lot of good is going to happen to you."

When Elly confided in her mother about this experience, her mother became very upset. "Elly, what am I going to do with you? You have such a vivid imagination."

Nearly sixty years later Elly could still recall the details of that childhood vision. "I can still recall the feeling I had when I heard that voice and when I saw that airplane. I felt good about it."

When Elly was seven her mother became pregnant again.

"This time I'll get my boy," Christian boasted firmly.

"The stork is going to bring our family a new baby," Elna explained to Elly. "If you want a brother, put a piece of sugar in the window with a light blue ribbon. If you want a sister, put a red ribbon with the sugar." Later Elly noticed that her father ate the sugar. Why? Elly was full of questions.

Shortly before the baby's arrival, Elly's beloved grandmother died. "Grandmother has gone to heaven," Christian intoned piously.

"But if Grandmother has gone to heaven, why did they put her deep into the ground? Why did they cover her grave with flowers?" Elly had an insatiable curiosity. She always noticed everything and asked many questions, but she did not always get answers that satisfied her. A gnawing hunger persisted in her heart.

When the time for the baby's birth arrived, Elly's grandfather took her to visit an uncle. Two days later her grandfather returned with the news. "The stork has brought you a baby brother," he announced proudly.

How could the stork know anything about that? I saw my father eat that sugar, the little curly-haired girl wondered. But again Elly got no satisfying answers to her questions.

Abruptly Elly's world began to change rapidly. The baby brother, Mogen, was now the center of attention. "Isn't he cute!" one of the hotel guests gushed.

"This is my son," Christian announced proudly as he poured drinks for his friends.

"I can't listen right now, Elly. The baby is crying," the harried mother mumbled absent-mindedly as she rushed to change another diaper. "Will you shine Papa's shoes?"

Suddenly the cute, little strawberry blonde with the dancing feet was completely upstaged by a tiny, wrinkled, red-faced squawling bundle of trouble—a baby brother. But Papa and Mummy think he is a little bundle of joy, a little lamb, Elly thought.

Elly's Uncle Marius kept sheep on his farm—ordinary white sheep; none of them were black. When Elly got upset with her baby brother, Mogen, her father accused, "Well, Elly, you are the black sheep of this family!"

Later Elly told her schoolteacher, "My Uncle Marius has a big flock of sheep and they are *all* black sheep." Elly began to feel rejection keenly. Was she a black sheep? She did not want to be a black sheep. She did not like to be rejected. She wanted to be talented, beautiful, and special. Her heart longed to be more than the dancing daughter of a drinking bartender.

Elly was already an opinionated child. For example she did not like tea, althought her father enjoyed an early tea about five o'clock.

"Come on, Elly. I'll give you a prize. Just drink your tea," he coaxed, holding out a luscious chocolate eclair. Elly wanted the sweet very much. Cleverly she watched her father as she pretended to sip the tea. When his attention was diverted momentarily, Elly quickly poured the tea into one of her mother's flower pots.

"All done, Elly? That's a good girl. Here's your sweet." Christian never noticed Elly's prank but the flower knew. It began to droop!

After the baby brother so successfully captured center stage in the Hansen household, Elly lost all interest in food—especially split pea soup. She longed for love—not food.

"But, Elly, this is delicious soup. I had a nice piece of pork to boil with the yellow peas," her patient mother tried to entice her.

"She's so pale and she's losing weight."

"Well, we'll have to take her to the doctor," her parents decided. At the hospital a psychologist tried to help.

The head nurse thought that she could solve the problem. "Come, Elly, let's play," she persuaded in a friendly manner, but Elly still refused to eat. Finally, after Elly had once more vomited up her food, the exasperated nurse jerked the little girl into the bathroom, paddled her soundly, and insisted that she eat the regurgitated food.

Although she still hungered for more than food, Elly Hansen had met her match. From that day on she began to eat better.

Another paddling that Elly never forgot was over a tablecloth with red roses, green tassels, and a fringe. That fringe would make a nice collar for my dolly. There's so much of it that Mummy won't miss it, reasoned the mischievous little girl as she carefully cut off the fringe.

Mother Elna may have been quiet, but she was not stupid. "Elly Hansen, there is no one else in this house. You did it," she insisted when Elly denied her accusation. "A sound paddling and no supper!"

A friend had come over for a card game and heard Elly yelling during the spanking. Later he inquired, "Why were you howling so the last time I was here for a visit?"

"Me? Howling? Oh, that was the night I had such a toothache." Elly felt ashamed to admit how naughty she had been. She was beginning to develop a conscience along with her desire for attention, acceptance, and approval.

Fashionable ladies in elegant clothes often visited the hotel, and Elly envied them. One day a very beautiful lady wearing a broad-brimmed hat decorated with a big, red bow stopped to talk with her. When I grow up I want a hat just like that, Elly decided. She dreamed of growing up, becoming a lady, and wearing gorgeous clothes—of being important and loved.

Although Christian and Elna never took Elly back to church after she was christened, she did have a chance to go to Sunday school once when she was about ten years old. Her parents had been out half the night partying, but Mogen, a lively toddler, insisted on action early in the

21

morning. To keep peace in the house and let her parents sleep a while longer, Elly took Mogen for a walk.

"Where are you going, little girl?" a short, plump, middle-aged lady on her way to church stopped to question Elly.

"Nowhere special. I am just taking Mogen for a walk so he won't wake Papa."

"Would you like to go to church with me?" invited the kind woman with a sweet smile. For the first time Elly and Mogen went to Sunday school at a Baptist church. Elly never forgot the story she heard that morning. The teacher told an exciting story about a lamb, the Lamb of God. She also mentioned "cleansing blood." Then they all knelt for prayer.

One chance visit in an ordinary church left an indelible impression on the mind of this active, imaginative, inquisitive little girl. Were there answers to her questions? What was church all about? Who was this Lamb of God? Would He like a black sheep? But when Elly again asked Papa, "Can I go to Sunday school?" the answer was a resounding No. Christian had other plans for his daughter.

One day an American Dane drove up in a big, black Ford to register at the hotel. After watching Elly dance, he suggested, "Let me have this curly-topped dancing girl to take back to the United States." Although Christian Hansen would not agree to this unusual request, Elly thought it would be great to go somewhere in that big, black Ford.

"Why don't you let me go?" Elly teased.

"Well, you just don't know that big country of American. They could even sell you because you are pretty and blonde and white," her father warned soberly.

Who would buy little girls? Were little girls valuable?

"I would be all right. He's a Dane," Elly insisted, thinking she would be perfectly safe with a Dane even though he was a stranger. He likes me, she thought. It would be fun to go to American!

Although Elly did not go to America, she did enjoy visits to Copenhagen. Uncle William Flendtberg was a well-to-do businessman, a furrier, and Aunt Agnes was a generous, loving aunt. They bought Elly a doll.

"Oh, look! This dolly's eyes close. Look, Mummy, she has pretty little teeth." Although Elly loved dancing, swimming, and gymnastics, still she was all girl and loved baby dolls and mothering. Later, Aunt Agnes generously added a bed for the doll and also a pram (doll carriage).

Gifts from Aunt Agnes made Christmas special. Elly loved Christmas and as an adult always wanted to make Christmas joyous, especially for children.

After Elly started school she spent many holidays with the Flendtbergs in Copenhagen. Then another baby boy arrived. The Flendtbergs had a child, a fine, healthy boy named John. Once again Elly was upstaged by a baby boy.

Later two more little blonde, curly-haired girls, Kate and Lizette, completed the Hansen family. But Elly was the only redhead.

Denmark today

1. Rungsted, Elly Hansen's birthplace.
2. Frederiksvaerk, the Hansen's hometown.
3. Copenhagen, the capitol of Denmark where the university was located.

Chapter 2

....

"Repent!"

With two younger sisters as well as a brother, Elly spent much of her time babysitting. One day she pushed the pram with Baby Lizette down to a park filled with pine trees. Her friend Karen came along as well as Elly's other sister, Kate.

"Let's pretend we are Africans," Elly suggested. "We'll build our grass hut with these branches." She stuck smaller branches in her belt. "See my grass skirt! My shirt is made of grass, too. Africans live in grass huts." So the children played all day, pretending to be Africans.

At a young age Elly was aware of different people, different customs, bamboo huts, grass skirts, and faraway lands. Big ships owned by the old reliable East Asiatic Company docked in the harbor at Frederiksvaerk. Shipping was big business in Denmark, for Denmark served as a bridge between the rest of Europe and the Scandinavian countries.

Life had its bright spots, and Elly enjoyed school. "That Elly! Watch her hang by her toes on the trapeze," cried one of her friends. By the time she was seven Elly excelled in swimming and gymnastics.

Elly grew in knowledge as well as physically and socially. From grade four throughout high school she studied English as well as German. From the fifth grade to the seventh she studied the Scandinavian languages and French. In her last year of high school she took Latin.

Compulsory religious education also played a part in the school curriculum in Denmark. Although Elly never attended church, she did have Bible training in school. She studied the Lutheran catechism and enjoyed singing the melodious traditional hymns of the church. Unfortunately, after telling one of the Bible stories, her teacher remarked disdainfully, "Of course, I don't really believe that."

Always active and energetic, Elly became involved in Green Scouts. In this work she learned how to be alert and self-reliant in a forest, how to determine the direction in which the wind blew, and how to build an outdoor fire. "Observe everything. Find your own way," the leader instructed Elly as she left the scouts in the center of Copenhagen and told them to draw a map of where they had been.

Out in the woods the scouts constructed a rope bridge over water, climbed trees, and built an outdoor toilet. Elly loved it all. When she became a group leader she received a silver star.

"We will meet the queen at our next meeting. Elly, you will serve tea."

"Me?" Elly had rather climb a tree. Although she was

excited, she performed her hostess duties graciously.

Later she described the queen to her mother. "The queen was very sweet, Mother, but she had so much lipstick on." Elly was never a worldly or vain person and had little patience with those who were. Her mother talked of the queen's mother who lived in an old castle outside of town. The Danes were proud of their royal family.

From the time that Elly was about eleven, Christian began drinking and gambling more and more. About this time he promoted Elly to a more practical task in the hotel than dancer. He taught Elly how to mix drinks and tend bar. Ever curious, intelligent, and interested in people, Elly soon learned to entertain and proved to be a drawing card at the hotel. Christian realized this and utilized Elly's good looks, personality, and poise. "There is a worldwide depression on. Even in the United States people are hungry, selling apples on the street, and eating at soup kitchens. We must keep our business growing, Elly."

In 1935 teen-aged Elly continued studying catechism in preparation for confirmation in the Lutheran church. Pastor Graabaek, a committed, concerned Lutheran, conveyed to the young girl a desire to know more about the Lord.

Elly developed into a beautiful young lady interested in improving physically, mentally, and socially. One day she spotted a big hat in a shop window. "That is just like the hat I have always wanted," she cried. "I must have that elegant hat."

Her enthusiasm fizzled when her father saw the hat. "Why do you have to buy a hat as big as a mill wheel?"

he asked sarcastically.

"I like it," Elly insisted stoutly, but big hats and pretty dresses did not satisfy the hunger in her teen-aged heart. I'll start smoking, she decided. That's what grownups do. Elly began smoking at fourteen, but smoking did not assuage her spiritual hunger either.

"Papa, may I go to the YMCA for a meeting tonight?" Elly asked, thinking, The YMCA is not church, but it is a Christian organization. Perhaps I can get to know some good Christian young people at the YMCA.

"No," was the emphatic answer. "No church and no YMCA either." Thus Elly's life essentially still had no contact with church. But deep within, a desire for a different life continued to develop.

1937 came. Hitler was rearming Germany, and Denmark noticed. In Elly's home town marines marched again. In the summer the marines marched through town to lively band music. Every girl in town wanted to march with them.

"Elly, you are not to go flirting and marching with those soldiers." Christian Hansen well knew how soldiers behaved with pretty young girls.

One night the marines planned an exciting torchlight parade. Elly watched as the soldiers with smart uniforms with shining buttons and holding big torches marched briskly by. Since World War I Denmark had reduced its military forces and had fought worldwide depression and unemployment by state-backed projects such as roads and bridges. The Danes had also raised the standard of public schools considerably and created an excellent system of public libraries. Because of Hitler's emphasis on the military, they now began to rebuild their military bases, and the marines marched regularly.

One particular marine not only marched but also eyed Elly. Later he asked, "May I walk you home?"

Although Elly knew that she was not allowed to "march with the soldiers," this marine talked so nicely that Elly thought she would enjoy his company. "Well, we had better not stop out here. Let's walk over the hilltop. Then you can go back through the woods, and I'll go another direction."

But Christian Hansen saw Elly and the soldier, and he waited for her. "I thought I told you to leave those soldiers alone," he yelled, then slapped her on the cheek. "You are a bad girl. What did you do? Did he try anything?"

"No, Papa, we didn't even hold hands." Elly tried to explain, but all Christian wanted Elly to do was shine his shoes, tend bar, help with the housework, and baby-sit.

"We had to walk out of three homes with everything sold because of his gambling," Elly remembered. She desired something else, so as she pushed the pram with the youngest baby sister, she dreamed of the airplane and the voice which said, "You are a lucky little girl. Something good will happen to you."

One of Elly's best high school friends was Edith Jurgensen. Despite her work in the hotel, Elly and Edith found time for fun. Swimming, skating, dancing, knitting, and crocheting, as well as long sessions of "girl talk," filled their days.

Edith's family differed greatly from Elly's folks. They were strong church people but not Lutheran. The Jurgensens were part of the two percent of Danes who were not members of the state church. They attended the

Evangelical Gospel Church. This church even sent prospective missionaries to Moody Bible Institute in America for training.

Although her parents were deeply committed believers, Edith was still just a fun-loving girl not quite ready to follow Jesus completely.

"When I finish high school, I am going to Copenhagen to the university," Edith announced.

Elly had no immediate plans for her own future. Soon I'll be out of high school. What will I do? Where will I go? she wondered as she polished glasses and wiped off the bar for the hundredth time. Although she had no specific goals, Elly definitely desired something different. She wanted a challenge.

Just before the holidays in 1938, Edith invited Elly to a special Christmas service in her church. Without asking permission or mentioning her plans to her family, Elly decided to go to that service with Edith.

"Repent, for the kingdom of heaven is at hand," the pastor preached. Elly's heart hungered to know more about this message.

On Tuesday Edith again invited Elly to church, "We have a visiting pastor who is going to preach." Immediately Elly made up her mind to go to church again.

"Repent, for the kingdom of heaven is at hand," the visiting pastor's voice rang out loud and clear.

Isn't that strange! Both preachers preached from the same text. I wonder why? Was it just coincidence? The young Elly Hansen was puzzled.

"Don't forget to come next Saturday, Elly," reminded Edith. "They are having a special farewell service for me at the church. You are my best friend, so I want you to come. Our youth pastor will be preaching."

"I'll be there."

"Repent! The kingdom of heaven is at hand." The same text that the other two preachers had used rang in Elly's ears.

Whatever does it mean? Is God trying to tell me something? Elly was stirred deeply.

About eleven o'clock that night as the girls walked through the snow, a full moon shone through the bare branches of the trees.

"Have you ever repented, Edith?" Elly inquired of her friend.

"I am so young! I have hardly thought much about it."

"Don't you realize? We have heard three different preachers, and all three of them have been preaching the same words. Didn't you even notice?"

One thing was sure—Elly had noticed. When she reached the privacy of her bedroom, she knelt by her bed and began to talk to God.

"God, I want to repent. I'll stop smoking. I'll stop tending bar. Just show me, God, what you want me to do." What peace flooded her soul! The full moon shone brightly on the young girl's face as she slept the sleep of the repentant. God had heard her "sinner's prayer." Her hungry heart had tasted "honey in the rock," and this world could never satisfy her again.

The next morning about six o'clock, she came to the breakfast table where her father, her mother, and her two younger sisters sat. Usually she lit her first cigarette of the day at the breakfast table, but not this morning.

"I have decided to follow Jesus. I am going to stop smoking. I will not tend bar anymore. I don't want anything more to do with liquor or anything like that," the strong-willed young girl unflinchingly announced her decision. "I am going to follow Jesus."

Christian's mouth fell open. His face turned pale for a moment, then he shouted, "If you want to follow Jesus, well, follow Him. But not here!" He slammed his fist on the kitchen table as he yelled at his seventeen-year-old daughter, Elly. "If you want a home and want to be here, you cannot follow Jesus. Now make up your mind what you are going to do. Follow Jesus? Then pack your stuff and follow Him. See where He will lead you."

King Christian X on his daily horseback ride in Copenhagen.

Chapter 3
. . . .

Elly Chooses to
Follow Jesus

"I *will* follow Jesus!" Seventeen-year-old, red-headed Elly Hansen was just as determined as her stubborn father.

"Well, follow Jesus then! See where He will lead you. You have had your last meal here." Christian Hansen, who for some unknown reason was now totally anti-God and antichurch, watched angrily as his young daughter marched up to her bedroom, packed her bag, and left her home in his hotel. Never again would she dance to entertain and enchant his hotel guests. Never again would she tend bar at his hotel. Thirteen years passed before she ever crossed the threshold of her childhood home again. But when Elly left her home hungry for a deeper life that day, she had a strong, sweet assurance that God was with her. Later she affirmed, "I never once regretted my decision.''

Where will I go? What will I do? Questions flooded the young girl's mind. I certainly won't tend bar anymore—ever! First of all, I'll have to find a job. But what can I do? Bartending and baby-sitting are all I know.

Elly's concerns were valid. In the thirties a major economic crisis—depression—spread worldwide. Denmark had experienced more than one major crisis since World War I, but none as severe as the depression which struck in the 1930s. Consequently, Denmark desired the social development of its 4.5 million people. Along with the other Scandinavian countries, it had agreed on drastic disarmament.

Elly as well as the average Dane scarcely noticed the storm brewing in Europe. She had to find a place to live. "God, I don't know what to do. Will You help me?"

"Where are you going?" A soft voice interrupted young Elly's troubled thoughts.

"Why, Mrs. Fufk! Is it really you?" Astonished, Elly lifted her head and saw Mrs. Fufk, the same kind Baptist lady who had taken Mogen and her to Sunday school when she attended church once as a small child.

"Where am I going? I don't really know." Elly explained that her father had expelled her from her home because she had decided to follow Jesus.

"I have a house with several rooms. Go home with me, Elly. Then you can find work. But until you find the right job, you can stay with me." Agnes Fufk opened her heart and her home to the young girl who had been rejected by her own father because she hungered and thirsted after Jesus. So began Elly's first big lesson in faith. "My God shall supply all your needs through Christ

Jesus." And God did supply her needs, even during a depression.

"Where did you make your decision to follow Jesus, Elly?" queried Mrs. Fufk.

"At the Free Gospel Evangelistic Church," Elly responded.

"Well, it's up to you where you go to church, Elly. But I think you should go to the church where you met the Lord. I am Baptist but our church is on the other end of town." Thus the gracious Baptist friend kindly helped the young girl to follow Jesus but did not try to exploit her rejected condition or force her to join the Baptist church.

Despite the high unemployment rate Elly found a job. She kept in touch with her mother and visited with her, but not at her father's hotel. She soon made several friends and a place for herself at the Danish Free Gospel Evangelistic Church. "Elly, we need you to help us in Sunday school. Will you teach the boys and girls aged nine to fifteen?" Later the church workers took Elly to another Sunday school in a town twelve kilometers away.

Elly and her friends rode bicycles to these churches. Since 1890 bicycles had been common in Denmark and were a symbol of freedom for youth. Elly's robust health and hearty stamina stood her in good stead during the cold weather, snow and rain. Her heart bubbled with her newfound love for Jesus, and she willingly worked and witnessed for Him with greater zeal than she ever had danced or tended bar. Wherever and whenever there was a church service, Elly Hansen attended. With her first month's pay, she purchased a small, brown Danish Bible that she still has more than forty years later.

Sunday school teaching challenged Elly, but she still hungered for more. Already she heard an inner voice saying, "Elly, I want you to witness and work for me beyond the borders of Denmark. I want you to be a fisher of men." Every Dane knew about fishing, but what was a fisher of men?

Beyond Denmark? A fisher of men? A missionary? Does God want me to be a missionary?

As Elly prayed concerning this, suddenly she saw a copper red road winding through a dark green jungle. She saw a church with a cross on top at the end of the road. Then she heard a voice say, "I want you to be used of God."

A missionary? If I could go to the foreign field as a missionary perhaps that would satisfy this longing in my soul. The young girl pondered these things in her heart. Decisive, determined to follow Jesus, Elly began to dedicate her life fully to His will.

After asking a few questions about missionary work, Elly found out that even to be accepted as a candidate for the mission field with the Free Gospel Evangelistic Church, she needed training either as a doctor, a nurse, or a teacher. Further questioning disclosed that in Denmark a nurse's training was cheaper than a teacher's training.

Then I will study nursing, Elly decided, knowing full well that she herself would have to earn every bit of the money she needed for her education. She moved to Birkerod, a town about twenty kilometers from Copenhagen.

In Birkerod was a large state psychiatric hospital with two thousand male and two thousand female patients who were retarded but not violent. Thick woods surrounded the big complex, which included a large farm and a carpentry shop where the handicapped were taught to be as useful as possible. There Elly began training as a nurse. Her first evening studies at the university included psychology for mental patients. She continued to work during the days.

In nearby Germany, after the death of the aged Hindenburg, the chancellorship and the presidency merged, and Adolf Hitler consolidated his power over the country. Army officers and government officials now took the oath of allegiance to him personally. War clouds threatened Elly as well as many other young people all over the world but especially in that part of Europe.

Hitler's rise to power and the German rearmament spelled an immediate threat to Denmark. England indicated that the Danes could not depend on it and signed a naval agreement with Germany that conceded the Baltic Sea to Germany.

In May 1939, on German initiative, Denmark signed a nonagression pact with Germany and repeatedly assured Germany of its neutrality. Despite this action Germany secretly planned an invasion of Norway, known as Operation Weseruebung, and the control of Danish territory with its adjacent waters and air space was judged necessary to the success of that operation. The storm in Europe soon encroached upon Denmark.

When Hitler marched into Poland during September 1939, rationing of certain items such as sugar and coffee began in Denmark. The winter of 1940 blew in extremely cold, and ice blocked the Danish ports for a long time, which resulted in a shortage of raw materials, principally fuel. Spring introduced a new kind of cold!

April 9, 1940, was an unforgettable day for Denmark. At 4:00 a.m. German troops crossed the southern border of Denmark. More troops landed at a number of Danish ports, including Copenhagen, where they went ashore from a German merchant ship which had docked, unchallenged, at the central Langelinie Quay. Parachute troops dropped at strategic points, and bombers flew over Danish territory, threatening to bomb defenseless cities.

The German minister to Denmark handed the Danish government a memorandum demanding submission. Between 5:00 and 6:00 a.m. King Christian met with the members of the government in Copenhagen to consider the German demands.

"Emergency mobilization of our Danish forces is not now possible."

"Geographically we cannot hope to resist."

"Remember, Winston Churchill said in February that Britain cannot help us."

"We have no alternative but to yield to the German demands."

Then came the public proclamation: "The government has acted in the honest conviction that in so doing we have saved the country from an even worse fate. It will be our continued endeavor to protect our country and its people from the disasters of war, and we shall rely on the people's cooperation." At first the Danes were resigned to the occupation, but later their feelings, including Elly's, changed radically.

Copenhageners on their way to work that fateful morning found their way barred by heavily armed German troops. They were shocked and they offered silent resistance even then. The Germans commandeered every truck they could lay their hands on, but every firm in the capital was soon warned and kept its vehicles at home.

April 9, 1940, was Elly's day off. "Meet me at Mrs. Fufk's, Mummy," she had planned. Suddenly the sound of many people flooded the air.

"Who is that? What's going on?"

A storm of lean, hungry Nazi soldiers poured into the city. Abruptly they took over businesses, including eight newspapers, that had belonged to Jews. They appropriated large ships that had belonged to Jews, as well as trucks, cars, and other equipment. The thing Denmark had feared had come to pass. Hitler had occupied Denmark. The storm in Europe gathered momentum, engulfing many nations.

"Look, Mother! That Nazi soldier put his fist through that bakery, and he is eating the pastry!"

"How thin they are! Elly, they must be starved." The fresh fruit and vegetables, the country butter, and the delicious cheeses of Denmark tempted the German soldiers. Food was high on their list of priorities.

Immediately after the news of the German attack, the Danish ambassador to the United States, Henrik Kauffmann, declared himself a "free" Danish ambassador. Kauffmann thus did not feel bound by orders from Copenhagen but reserved his freedom to act in accordance with Denmark's true interests as he saw them. He requested the American government's endorsement of this standpoint and got it immediately.

"They didn't take over all our country," the news spread. The Faroe Islands and Greenland lay beyond German reach. British troops landed in the Faroes, and Kauffmann granted the United States bases in Greenland on his own responsibility. The Germans denounced the treaty as a breach of international law, but for months a handful of experienced Greenland Danes patrolled the great wastes of the east coast of Greenland, the largest island in the world, on one-man expeditions by dog sled. They located several German weather stations and relayed the information to the U.S. Air Force, which then destroyed the bases.

At the time of the occupation the greater part of the Danish merchant fleet, consisting of about two hundred ships with a tonnage of 1,100,000, sailed throughout the world and slipped out of German reach. Over the Danish radio the authorities ordered the crews of all ships to make for a neutral port, preferably Italian or Spanish. London radio appealed to them to proceed to Allied ports. More than ninety percent of the seamen (about five thousand men) chose to sail for an Allied port and join the war under the British flag. Six hundred paid for this decision with their lives, and sixty percent of the ships were sunk.

Also in April 1940 a Danish journalist named Ebbe Munck heard the news of Denmark's occupation in Finland, where he was serving as a war correspondent. Concerned for his country's international reputation, Munck returned to Denmark, secretly contacted officers of the military intelligence, and discovered that they agreed with him. He got himself appointed as his paper's correspondent in Stockholm in order to collect information systematically about German ship and troop movements. Then he transmitted this material to Britain. The Resistance movement quickly developed leaders.

Although the Germans were noticeably thin and

undernourished, the Danes, including Elly, had little sympathy for the arrogant, goose-stepping soldiers of the Third Reich.

I wish I could put my fist in his face, thought many a sullen, angry Dane as the Nazis continued to plunder, commandeer, and exploit businesses. But the tight Danish fists were clenched helplessly in their pockets.

"There was little that we could do but give the Germans the cold shoulder," Elly later recalled. The "cold shoulder" was a new "secret weapon" that the Danes employed to perfection during the occupation. Although it was a severe test of self-control, it was just a matter of pretending that the "Herrenvolk" did not exist.

In September 1942 King Christian celebrated his seventy-second birthday. Hitler sent him a 165-word congratulatory telegram. The king's brief reply, "Express my best thanks," infuriated Hitler. He was so angry that he forced the Danish prime minister to resign. From the King to the lowliest laborer the Danes continued to use the "secret weapon." Gradually resistance began to grow.

The story was whispered all over Copenhagen of the little milk boy who was stopped by a German soldier as he delivered milk at the doors. The soldier had noticed that King Christian took his daily horseback ride apparently without a bodyguard.

"Who watches your king?" the soldier asked threateningly, remembering how closely Hitler was guarded.

The milk boy stood tall and replied firmly, "We all do!" The Danes did watch their beloved king with pride. Just a few days after the German occupation he calmly resumed his daily horseback rides through the streets of Copenhagen with no protection but the general public.

The spontaneous homage shown to King Christian X by his subjects was a pointed demonstration of the Danish determination not to be daunted on their own ground.

Responsible persons said that the king promised to wear the Jewish star if it was introduced in Denmark by the Germans during the war. The Germans, foreseeing complications, never forced the Danish Jewish citizens to wear the star as was done in Germany and other occupied countries. Indeed King Christian exercised his royal status and personal influence, not only to protect his Jewish subjects, but to mitigate the conditions of Jews elsewhere.

"Diesem lacherlichen Landchen" ("this ridiculous little country") was the German reaction. But daily the determination of the citizens of "this ridiculous little country" began to mount. Isolated they were, but information managed to filter in.

In 1940 ten acts of sabotage occurred. An underground newspaper began to flourish with a circulation of twelve hundred. Resistance began to stiffen.

In February 1941 the Danish underground expanded its contacts for gathering intelligence and improved a courier service between Denmark and the free world via Sweden. At the same time preparations were made in Britain to dispatch the first parachute agents to Denmark. An invitation was sent to Christmas Moller, a Conservative party member, to come to London. The plan was for this distinguished politician, an outspoken anti-German who had been forced out of the government, to lend his authority to the Danish Resistance at home and abroad. Moller took the ferry into Sweden, then went on to London.

April 9, 1941 was the first anniversary of the German occupation. "Remember, girls, two minutes of silence at noon!" the word was passed around in Elly's school. All work and all traffic came to a halt. Town Hall Square in Copenhagen was crowded with patriots of the "ridiculous little country." Resistance slowly increased. In 1941 there were nineteen acts of sabotage. The underground newspaper circulation increased to 40,000.

At the nurse's school Elly and the loyal Danish nurses decided that they were not going to let time just pass. "There must be something we can do," insisted Elly. Unafraid, Elly remembered that her father and her grandfather had both served in the Danish military. Patriotic and loyal, Elly loved her country and King Christian X. She joined the Resistance.

Round Tower and Trinity Church, hiding place for the Torah scrolls, 1943–45.

Gilleleje Church in north Zealand, hiding place for many Danish Jews as they escaped to Sweden and freedom.

The escape to Sweden: a refugee is helped up from the hold.

Chapter 4
· · · · · · · · · · · · ·

Love and War

In 1942 Christmas Moller, now in Britain, and speaking over the British Broadcasting Corporation network, appealed for an active Danish contribution in the form of sabotage. The number of acts of sabotage rose dramatically to 122. People continued to read the underground newspaper. Circulation increased to 301,000 that year.

But all was not anxiety and talk of war. Romance blossomed when Elly, now twenty-one, hurried back to the hospital in Birkerod. Late in the evening she came through the tunnel to get up to the street to catch a bus. A young man approached her, saying he lived not far away from the hospital. As they walked he told Elly about his farm where he planted shrubbery. "My father owns this bus company, too. I know your father, Christian Hansen."

After the couple boarded the bus they continued talking. "I'd like to come by the hospital to see you, and we'll go for a walk."

Later Elly told the hospital matron about her new friend.

"That's nice. I'm glad you have found a friend."

The young man, whom we shall call Karl, sent Elly gifts of flowers and chocolates. The young couple continued to take walks and occasionally went for boat rides. "He's getting serious," the other nurses teased Elly. Elly soon realized that indeed Karl was serious. After her twenty-first birthday in July 1942, Karl surprised her with an engagement ring on August 12. "I think we should get married around Christmas," Karl proposed.

Elly returned to her church in her home town for a prayer meeting. As she sought God, He reminded her of her call to the mission field. Karl is not even a member of the church, she remembered. And he smokes, too.

For three months Elly and her friends at church prayed. You are about to step out of My will, God whispered to her heart, Don't forget your desire to follow Me. Aren't you determined to dedicate your life to missions?

The next time Karl came to visit Elly she told him, "I cannot marry you, Karl. I have a call to the mission field. You are not a Christian. It would never work."

"Well, to let you know that I am true to what I have proposed to you, Elly, I'll give up smoking. I'll go to church sometimes, and I would never stand in your way. You have a right to follow your heart's desire."

But Elly had a strong feeling that marriage to Karl was outside the will of the Lord. "I have made a wrong step, Karl. You must forget about me. You will meet another girl that just might be the right one for you."

The experience left its mark on Elly as she saw the disappointment on Karl's face when she returned his rings. Engagement promises are not to be played with, she decided. I had given my word to Karl and I had received his rings. I won't do this again. I am determined to give my life one hundred percent for the Lord. An engagement should be just as holy as a marriage. That was a wrong step. I must follow Jesus.

Despite war and wartime romances and marriages, Elly still determined to dedicate herself to His call. She clung closer to the church, and despite her infant baptism as a Lutheran, she felt that she should be baptized by immersion, so she was baptized in the North Sea when she was twenty-one.

Elly's decision concerning Karl displeased her father. Christian knew Karl's well-to-do family and liked the idea of having such a son-in-law. He and Karl met in bars on occasion and discussed the family and the farm. Once again the strong-willed father and the committed Christian daughter differed, and the estrangement between them deepened.

Karl respected Elly's decision, but he could not forget her. But I must follow Jesus, Elly decided. "No more wrong steps." And she never regretted her decision.

In the fall of 1942, after the birthday greeting "cold shoulder incident," the Danish government was reshuffled. A different German plenipotentiary (administrator) arrived in November, and he argued with Berlin for a more lenient course. Berlin agreed to allow an ordinary general election in March 1943. This resulted in a tremendous turnout at the polls which crushed a couple of small pro-Nazi factions and united the population in their resistance against Germany.

A British air raid on one of the biggest Copenhagen factories in January 1943 was welcomed despite unavoidable Danish casualities. In the first four months of 1943 the acts of sabotage numbered fourteen, twenty-nine, sixty, and seventy. More than five hundred underground newspapers continued to flourish with a combined circulation of 2,600,000 in 1943. At the same time friction between the German troops and the population became more frequent and more serious. From the king to the smallest, most insignificant peasant, Danes were bent but not broken, occupied but not conquered. This "ridiculous little country" was a survivor!

After three years in Birkerod, Elly went back to her home town of Fredriksvaerk to begin medical training in her nursing program. Three more years and an exam each year, she thought. I will still have a year in midwifery, then more training with the mentally disturbed. The young girl decided upon this long, hard, strenuous program and rededicated herself to follow Jesus. She felt confident that He would take care of her even during the stress of wartime. The discipline required not only to survive but to continue her education put steel in Elly's character. God was carefully grooming her for a life that would challenge her to the utmost.

The large hospital in Frederiksvaerk served Denmark's only steel-rolling mill, founded in 1756. Water power from the biggest Danish lake, Arreso, helped in the manufacture of cannons, cannonballs, and gunpowder. The mill ran full blast to fill war orders. The hospital staff reserved fifty percent of the hospital beds for the steelworkers. Accidents, especially burn cases, often occurred in the steel mill.

Now twenty-one, Elly dedicated herself to her goal. Her duties and responsibilities as a nurse kept her running so that she often took the stairs two at a time. Although Elly occasionally met her mother, she still felt that her family did not understand or appreciate her desire to follow Jesus.

In the meantime the Nazis were openly trying to solve the "Jewish problem" in Copenhagen. Elly saw them drag elderly Jewish women by their hair down flights of stairs. They occupied Jewish homes, throwing fine furniture out of second-floor and third-floor windows to the ground, then setting fire to it.

Most of the Danish people bitterly resented such brutality. In every town in Denmark people worked in the underground to spoil the work of the Germans and hinder them. In July there were 84 acts of sabotage, 198 in August.

Copenhagen, the countryside, and the coast were patrolled by the Germans, but just a few miles across the sea the lights of neutral Sweden beckoned. In October 1943 a few Jewish familes were able to make their way as normal travelers on the ferries which still sailed, under observation, to Sweden. But the great majority had to be hidden over a period of days before they could be smuggled to the fishing ports. Danish doctors, nurses (including Elly), and other medical personnel played an important role, registering refugees in their hospitals and clinics under assumed names, then transporting them in ambulances and even in mock funeral corteges.

In the hospital where Elly was training, a group of courageous, imaginative nurses formed an underground resistance group. "Whatever is useful to them, let's destroy," one girl suggested.

"Hide our bread deep in the cellar," another added.

"I just can't bear the way those Nazis are treating the Jews," another said angrily. Copenhagen, with its one million people, was surrounded by small towns, and an escape route for Jews began to emerge.

"If we could just get the Jews to come here to this coastal town, perhaps we could smuggle them on into Sweden."

"If they rode the very last electric train from Copenhagen," Elly suggested.

"Oh, yes, it would be hard to watch that train," another chimed in.

"Caution them to go to Holti. I hear that station is especially poorly guarded." The nurses planned and watched, observed and hoped, and then began to get more actively involved.

"We need a password for Jews," someone decided.

"Lemon! Let's call the Jews lemons."

It was agreed. Soon the telephone calls began to trickle in. "Could you please pick up a dozen lemons tonight at ten o'clock?" Often they picked up their "lemons" during the rush hour, then took them to a home that was cooperating with them there in Holti.

"But the curfew? How can we manage the curfew?" someone questioned.

"Well, since I work here in this hospital, I am allowed out after curfew," Elly reminded. "I can ride my bicycle to Holti, walk these people through the woods, get them into a car early in the morning, and drive them to that church we have been told about!"

Churches, including the massive Grundtvig Church, were strong in their denunciation of Nazism and in their support of the Jews. Round Tower and Trinity Church hid Torah scrolls from 1943 to 1945.

The pastor of the church where Elly's resistance group wanted to hide their "lemons" joined in on the scheme. In fact he arranged for as many as 250 Jews to stay hidden in the church basement. But to get them on a fishing boat and over into Sweden was another problem. "What will we do about the German patrols?"

"Oh, no problem!" Elly knew how to entertain men. After all she had been a barmaid for years. She knew how to talk to lonely soldiers.

"We'll enchant those German soldiers. They are lonely. They know everybody hates them, and they are starved for home cooking. Let's bake cookies and make coffee. We'll have a beach party."

"I'll make cookies. Shall I put poison in them?"

"I can play my guitar," offered Elly.

Then one of the men of the church spoke up. "If you girls can entertain those nasty Nazi soldiers, then perhaps we can get some boats and get those poor Jews on the boats."

"I know a fisherman who will bring his boat. It holds fifty." So the Danes planned and worked.

Although they despised the conquering German soldiers, the ingenuous nurses hid their distaste and did what they detested, turned a soft answer to wrath, and responded pleasantly to insolences. Thus they were able to save the lives of thousands of Danish and German Jews. The Jews never forgot this kindness, and in 1980 Elly saw the monument to the Danes' courage and kindness which stands in Jerusalem.

Not all Jews, escaped, however. Rumors began to float about in Denmark about death camps in Germany and Poland. Occasionally exhausted German soldiers came over to Denmark from the front lines in France, Holland, and Russia for rest and relaxation but most of all for food.

The early summer of 1943 saw a nationwide wave of sabotage. Whole towns went on a demonstrative strike in which all work stopped and only the most vital public services were maintained. Emotions were at fever pitch. The top German administrator was recalled to Berlin to the Fuhrer's headquarters. On August 28, the Danish government was given an ultimatum which demanded the introduction of the death penalty for sabotage, the declaration of martial law throughout the country, a total ban on strikes and meetings, and direct German censorship.

The Danish government, with full approval of the king, rejected this ultimatum, and during the night, the German military took over executive power. In the early hours they made widespread arrests of hostages throughout the country and without warning disarmed the Danish garrisons. The navy managed to scuttle its ships. The Danish government ceased to exist.

In October 1943 Berlin ordered the arrest of all Danish Jews. Jews were warned, concealed, and conveyed to Sweden in a swiftly organized, large-scale operation. The action was strongly supported in Sweden, where with government approval, refugee organizations were set up, on Swedish soil with full-time officers. Under pressure and chaotic conditions about 7000 persons escaped. Only about 450 were arrested and taken to Germany. "These people are involved in underground activity," the Germans accused as they arrested policemen, doctors, pastors, and many others.

"Do be careful, Elly," people warned. "You nurses must be very careful. You will get arrested and sent to Germany if they ever discover what you are doing."

Elly still roomed with her Baptist friend, Mrs. Fufk. Any time she was off work the Fufk home was her home. The Fufks were also a part of the underground. The Resistance movement continued and organized itself as the Freedom Council in September. The underground press continued to break through the censorship. News of the progress of the war was common talk.

"If the Nazis find out that you have that gun, Elly, you may get shot."

"Better to be shot than sent to one of those awful death camps in Germany," Elly retorted as she slipped a sharp knife in her pocket. "I'll take this box of pepper, too. Pepper in the eyes will stop anyone." Ever resourceful and self-reliant, Elly determined to trust in God but to keep her powder dry! God helps those who help themselves, Elly decided, as she kept thinking of other ways to help defeat the enemy.

Another interesting facet of the work at her hospital concerned the social rehabilitation of "girls of the street." The Danish government worked through the local police force, arrested the girls, and placed them in a nurse's training program. The goal was to redirect their lives so that they could be able to function in society in a normal, helpful way. When these girls completed their nurse's training, they were able to earn good wages in a socially accepted profession. Thus Elly and the other nurses had access to police training including karate and gun training—useful skills in the underground movement.

The Danes noticed who helped in the Resistance movement and who did not. "What about that Inga? Is she with us or is she actually flirting with that German soldier?"

"Well, if she is really sweet on him, we can make her very sweet and attractive indeed." The fiercely patriotic nurses wreaked havoc on any would-be collaborating sweetheart. They rolled more than one little flirt in syrup, flour, and feathers. In order to hide their identity the vengeful nurses pulled stockings over their faces, blind-folded the German soldiers' Danish girlfriend, and then proceeded with the punishments.

"She ought to be grateful we didn't scratch her eyes out, that disloyal hussy!"

"She is just a traitor that's all!"

The life physician of the king, Professor Wuarberg, was a Jew who hid in the hospital in Birkerod when Elly was in training. Every morning Elly brought him coffee and breakfast down in the basement where he was con-ducting his research on the brains of patients who had died in the hospital. He was one of the top men in medicine in Denmark. He survived the war and later repaid Elly's kindness in a most significant way.

By 1944 the war was very fierce. The king was im-prisoned in his own palace. Resistance became increas-ingly effective all over Europe. The Germans took violent countermeasures, including random shootings—often of well-known persons—arrests, deportations, and execu-tions, but these proved useless against the Resistance. In the summer of 1944 German violence sparked off a total general strike in Copenhagen that completely paralyzed the large city for a week.

On September 19, in a surprise action all over the country two thousand out of nine thousand Danish policemen were arrested and transported to German concentration camps. Most of the other policemen went underground. The autumn of 1944 and the winter of 1945 saw an increased number of sabotage actions, along with an influx of 250,000 refugees from eastern Germany.

In the spring of 1945, 200,000 German soldiers were on guard duty in Denmark. The Resistance movement furnished the British Royal Air Force with scale models of the Gestapo headquarters in Copenhagen, and on March 21, 1945, it was destroyed in a low-level air attack along with the headquarters at Arhus and Odense.

In the hospital where Elly trained, the head doctor, Dr. Jeans Gram, worked with the underground along with the nurses. Occasionally English pilots parachuted down over Denmark with weapons to aid the underground workers. Elly and the nurses hid one English pilot, Paul, right in the hospital. He had lost his copilot, and he himself had to have his legs amputated.

"Wouldn't it be wonderful if we could get word to that pilot's wife in England? If she could be here, it would be such a blessing to him."

"He says that his wife is expecting a baby soon."

The courageous Danes worked out the details and got word to London. Immediately the concerned English wife booked passage to Sweden and from there slipped into Denmark to be with her husband. Shortly after she arrived her husband died. One week later the young widow gave birth to Paul's son, little Paul. But the storm that had engulfed Denmark for five years was almost over. Before long patriotic Danes, including Elly, could lay down their weapons, pick up their lives, and get on with their dreams.

At the end of April 1945 Hitler committed suicide and the Allied forces reached Hamburg and Lubeck. On May 4 at 8:34 p.m., just when the Danish news bulletin was on the air from the BBC, the announcer stopped and said, "We have just received an important message. Allied Headquarters has announced that the German troops in northwest Germany, Holland, and Denmark have surrendered."

Elly and her fellow countrymen poured into the streets rejoicing. Church bells rang and streamers fluttered. Confetti filled the air.

The Danish flag with the white cross on red bunting, said to have dropped from heaven in 1211 and the oldest flag in Europe, flew briskly in the sea breeze.

All over Denmark, loyal Danes like Elly Hansen had taken many risks to help the Allies and do all they could to hinder the Nazis. For years afterward, Elly and most Danes just felt empty when German names were called.

Twenty-five years later, after Elly had been a missionary in Thailand for years, she found that she still had some strong feelings about the German people that she had to overcome.

Chapter 5

From London to Thailand

On May 5, 1945, King Christian X, who had been a prisoner in his own palace since September 1944, asked the former prime minister, V. Buhl, to form a new government. Denmark was free again.

The war delayed Elly but she utilized the long years to train as a nurse, sharpen her sickle and strengthen her courage. She never lost sight of her goal to be a missionary.

Elly finished her education as a first class nurse in Denmark in the later part of 1949, but she still had to go for further schooling with the Danish Mission Forbund, a missionary society connected with the China Inland Mission.

Should she go to Sweden, or would it be better to go to England for this training? Finally she decided to go to London Bible College in the north end of London. In her late twenties, after six years of medical training plus all the work in the underground during World War II, Elly looked forward to the Bible studies and a change of scenery.

Although she had worked for part of her education in Denmark, Elly went to London believing that if God had called her He would also provide her needs. Her home church and friends in Denmark felt obligated to help her, but they made no specific promises. "I am going without a promise, but I know God never fails." And He did not fail. All her needs were supplied. The faith that had filled Elly's heart at seventeen when she first said "I will follow Jesus" still flooded her soul with a sweet peace.

"Soon I'll begin my real missionary work. I just hope my English is good enough." The Danish nurse packed her bags.

When she arrived in London and tried to use her school English, the people just stared at her and complained, "We can't understand you." Although despair settled in on her, Elly soon made friends with the lady of the house where she boarded. Early every morning about four o'clock Elly could hear the dear woman pray, "O God, do help Elly Hansen with her English." The heating system acted like a microphone, and the prayer winged its way throughout the house and on to heaven. Three short months later Elly passed the English language courses and looking forward to her Bible classes.

In the missionary training home, Elly had to learn to eat the English way, then the Chinese way. Any prospective missionary to China had to learn to eat Chinese-style, to learn about the culture, and to learn a little of the language.

As an efficient, experienced, hard-working nurse, Elly

was used to a full, fast-paced life. Shortly after she settled in, a voice called downstairs, "Elly, would you please
come down here?" She got a lecture on how to behave
as a lady—how to walk, how to sit. There was to be no
more jumping down the stairs two at a time. How am I
ever going to learn all this English, Chinese, Hebrew, and
Greek plus all these Bible studies if I don't rush and run
as fast as I can? she wondered. But every time she ran
up the stairs she got a lecture on how a lady walks. "Also,
girls, when you dine, remove your chair quietly from the
table. Sit down as a lady, get up as a lady, and put your
chair back in place with *no* noise. We have very high-class
visitors here. The Hudson Taylor family and others with
higher social standards visit us. So you must learn how
to conduct yourselves as ladies." All the fuss and feathers
scarcely appealed to a Resistance nurse.

Elly had only been in London for three months when
she was sent out to speak at gospel meetings. "You may
go with Goodren, Elly." But Goodren confided, "You must
speak, Elly. I am scared to death. My knees start knock-
ing when I even testify."

The nurse who had survived a terrible war did not
lack courage. "Well, my English may be broken, but I
love the Lord and He will help me." So Goodren and Elly
began to conduct gospel meetings. After about nine
months Goodren began to take care of a meeting herself.
Later she married and went to Japan as a missionary.

The next year Elly moved to a coeducational training home. The women lived on the third floor, and the
men occupied the second floor, while the staff stayed on
the first floor. The building was carefully arranged with
no connection between the men's quarters and the

women's. The first class included twenty-six girls from all over Europe—Sweden, Germany, Norway, Denmark, France, and Switzerland. Most of the young people planned to enter missionary service, and a good many achieved that goal. Some went to Japan, some to the Philippines, and others to Singapore, but Elly felt a call to China. Would she ever reach China? She knew she must keep her nets cleaned and mended if she was to become a fisher of men, so she studied, prayed, and learned to trust God.

One lesson in trust Elly never forgot. "Trust God to supply your needs. Tell Him what your needs are. Don't ask others, ask Him." The teachers at London Bible School hammered this lesson home over and over. "Our financial policy is very simple. Every missionary must learn to look only to God for all his or her financial needs. No one is ever to state from a public platform that they need money for support, travel, or outfit. No letter is ever to be sent asking for financial aid of any sort. Finances are not to be mentioned except to praise God for providing."

"We shall be closing the training home for one month of vacation." Elly heard the news from Mrs. Frazier, a former missionary to the Lishui tribe in China. But where was she to go? What could she do? She did not have one penny.

"Where are you going, Elly?"

"I don't know. I am praying about it," she answered. She continued to talk to God about this need.

On Friday before leaving on Saturday night a Swedish lady telephoned. "I need four girls to stay in my place in Brighton for one month. I will send money for their train fare and expenses. My refrigerator is full of food. My caretaker will prepare their meals and give them what help they need."

Elly enjoyed a great vacation at Brighton, all provided by God. The home by the sea was like a castle with a marble staircase, elegant china, heavy silver, and crisp, fine linen. Thick bear skins covered the polished floors and silk spreads adorned the beds.

Two English girls and an Ethiopian princess shared the home with Elly. "Brighton is special. This is the home of the Hudson Taylor family."

"Yes, have you been to see his daughter? She always wants to visit with the candidates to China. She must be almost ninety!"

Later Elly went with the Ethiopian princess, who was studying nursing, to see about the girl's birth certificate.

"Where were you born, miss?" the official inquired.

The princess had difficulty with official papers but none whatsoever with witnessing. "Well, there may be some difficulty about my birth certificate but this I do know. I have been born twice," the princess testified to the astonished official. After a month's rest and recreation the four girls headed back to London for more class work.

On Sunday the students helped in the churches. Because of her nursing background, Elly went to Bethany Hospital and St. Mary's Hospital to give messages to the patients as they came for treatment. She also enjoyed going to a little mission church in the east end of London. The men students escorted the girls to these places around London.

Friendships developed normally. One day a young

man named Isaac who had a preaching engagement needed a favor. "Elly, could you please iron one of my shirts
for me? I really need to study my Bible a bit more for this
service."

"Sure, I'll help you out," Elly replied as she reached
for the shirt and started for the laundry.

While Elly was pressing the shirt, Mrs. Taylor (one
of the Hudson Taylor family who was in charge) came
down. "Elly, are you ironing a man's shirt?"

"Yes," Elly answered, wondering what was wrong.

"You are not to do that," Mrs. Taylor declared firmly.
"You are just not to do that."

Always practical, Elly wondered, What harm can
there be just from ironing a man's shirt? The nurse who
had attended male and female psychiatric patients and
rescued Jews from arrogant Nazi military men thought
ironing a man's shirt was very innocuous and certainly
innocent, but Elly obeyed those in charge. Well, most of
the time.

As young men and women will, the Bible School
students soon found a way to communicate between
floors, although they were strictly forbidden to use the
stairs. The stairs creaked noisily, so that someone in
charge always caught them anyway when they tried to
sneak onto a forbidden floor. The girls on the third floor
rigged up a dumb waiter (a small elevator) of sorts with
ropes in order to send coffee and cakes down to the boys.
"Elly, what in the world are you doing?" Sure enough,
Elly was caught.

Then there was the matter of the cheese from Denmark that Elly enjoyed so much. "What is that awful
odor?" Mrs. Taylor complained. "Elly, are you sneaking

in that dreadful cheese again? You know that cheese has a terrible odor." Mrs. Taylor had a very sensitive nose.

An innocent little canary caused the biggest ruckus of all. Mrs. Taylor had bought the canary. "It's a male bird," the sales clerk assured her.

But one morning an egg appeared in the cage. "Elly, why did you put that egg in my canary's cage?"

"What egg? I didn't put an egg anywhere. I don't know what you are talking about. I am trying to show my friend how to repair the inner tube on her bicycle. I am not bothering your canary." Mrs. Taylor was not convinced.

When the second egg appeared Mrs. Taylor was really upset and again accused Elly. "But Mrs. Taylor, I did not do that. I did not even think of such a trick. I could have done it but I did not. Don't you think your canary could be a lady instead of a boy?"

"Oh, no! I bought this canary myself, and the sales clerk told me that it was a male. Someone is trying to make fun of me." By the time the canary began to set on the eggs and then produced three more small eggs, Mrs. Taylor finally reluctantly admitted that her gentleman bird was indeed a lady canary.

Serious political repercussions caused more lasting disturbance than cheeses and canaries. The doors to China, the land of Elly's calling, slammed shut firmly. "Examine yourselves, students. Do you really have a call or not? There will be many problems for which you will need answers. Think and pray about where God wants you to go. Also, let your missionary board back home advise you as to where you should go."

After Elly completed her first year examination,

Pastor Elton from a small town in the south invited her for a weekend. This village church was in a farming area. "The pastor has a daughter who is a missionary in Ethiopia. The little Anglican church is very formal—high church—so be careful how you conduct yourself," Mrs. Taylor advised Elly. When the pastor asked her to come to the pulpit to speak, Elly felt a bit anxious but honored to help in any way she could.

Later she went out into the countryside and climbed a hill carrying her Bible. "God, I need an answer. What am I to do? Where do You want me to go? I thought I was called to China. For years I have studied and prepared myself for that place, and now the door to China is closed. I need a word from You, Lord." Wild daffodils covered the hills and little rabbits scampered to and fro. The serene setting calmed Elly's mind and after a time of prayer she heard from heaven. The Lord whispered to her heart: I want you to go to Siam. The daffodils swayed in the breeze, and the bunnies played hide-and-seek around their holes, but the beauty of hearing directly from God left a lasting impression on Elly.

A confirmation came when she contacted the mission board back in Denmark. She wrote a letter telling the board about the new leading from the Lord and mailed it by ship across the North Sea. Another ship sailed west carrying a letter from the board with a similar message. When Elly got the board's letter, she cried, "Those ships must have passed each other in the North Sea. This is the confirmation that I need to go to Siam."

Indeed Siam (now called Thailand) was a needy field. Ninety percent of the Thai people are Buddhist. Buddhism was introduced 2,300 years ago during the third century before Christ after Indian Buddhist Emperor Asok (267–227 B.C.) dispatched missionaries to southeast Asia to propagate the newly established faith. About four percent of Thais are Islamic, and only one-half percent are Christians of any kind. Yes, Thailand was in need of Christian missionaries.

In the meantime, missionaries coming out of China were not being sent anywhere else. The mission board appointed Elly as a pioneer missionary but the Danish director of foreign missions explained, "We don't quite know how we are going to work this out yet." Later he met a missionary who had already been in Thailand. As they talked about Thailand and the missionary work, Elly's director said, "We have a young nurse in training in the China mission just at this time, but of course, that is closed now. We just had a letter from her asking about Thailand. Our board feels that perhaps this might be the best place for her." Plans were made for Elly to go to Thailand with the Worldwide Evangelistic Crusade from the United States. Her first two years in Thailand were under their leadership.

She finished her training in England and returned to Denmark to work in her old hospital in order to raise the money for traveling. "Certainly, Elly, you can have a job. How about night matron?"

Although Elly was delayed in reaching the mission field, she still felt the hand of God on her life and continued to pray and work and save her money for her ticket to Thailand.

In 1951, thirteen years after Elly's father had demanded that his daughter leave home, Christian Hansen asked that she return.

"Your father is sick, Elly. He has to have an operation. It's his kidneys." Elly's nursing skills were very welcome as the operation was extensive and included repair for ulcers.

She was glad to help her father, but home still did not satisfy her hungry heart. "I have to finish my education, Papa. I am determined to be a missionary. My life is dedicated to Jesus."

Christian Hansen felt Elly's education would be much more valuable helping her family. "You're the oldest. You owe it to your family to help out."

One night when Elly came on duty at the hospital the daughter of one of the members in her church was brought in deathly sick. Elly called Dr. Enger Krog, but when the lady doctor arrived to examine the little girl lying on the table she said sadly, "We don't have anything to help this girl."

"She is the only child of her parents, and they cannot have any more children. We must pray. I believe in prayer," Elly declared firmly.

"You do?" cried the doctor as her eyes lighted up.

"I do! Let's pray." Elly laid her hands on the child, and the Lord healed her.

This excited the doctor so much that she took the girl back into the ward where eight older women patients were. "God has performed a miracle," declared the doctor. That night four of the ladies turned to God, and the doctor became a very close friend of Elly's. Elly's faith soared as she saw the miraculous healing power of God that night for the first time.

One day near the Christmas of 1951 Dr. Krog asked Elly, "Have you been baptized in the Holy Ghost?"

"I must have the Holy Ghost, or I wouldn't be able to get a true understanding of the Bible. So I suppose I have," Elly replied.

"Have you spoken in other tongues?"

"No," Elly answered. "And I'm not sure that I am supposed to. I think that is a thing of the past." The young graduate from London Bible School thought she was giving an intelligent answer, but Dr. Krog continued to talk about receiving the Holy Ghost although both professionals knew they were not supposed to become emotional on the job over religious issues.

"Do you dare to go to Thailand without the power of the Holy Ghost, speaking in other tongues?" questioned the doctor.

In 1952 the Reverend Rolstu Petersen, superintendent of the mission board, ordained Elly as a pastor. Later Elly thought more about her conversation with Dr. Krog. She began to speak to the Lord about it. "God, if You have anything special for me, and if it is the matter of the baptism of the Holy Ghost, speaking in other tongues—well, I know that everything from You is good so I want it."

Elly had many years of academic study in several areas, but she was open to truth and really wanted to understand more about the Lord. She was not quick to accept just anything, however. For about six months she prayed and prayed about receiving the Holy Ghost. Then one glorious day—May 12, 1952—Elly Hansen received her personal Pentecost, the baptism of the Holy Ghost with the sign of speaking in other tongues.

Much of the money that Elly earned in the hospital in Denmark was sent to the mission board each month to apply to her fare to Thailand. At last the great day arrived. Elly, now thirty-one years old, at last ordered her ticket on a Danish ship owned by the reliable East Asiatic Company, which had ships scheduled from Denmark to Thailand. The phone rang. "Miss Hansen, will you please send in the money by telegram for your ticket. We have scheduled your departure date." Immediately Elly called the secretary in charge of accounts and asked him to send the money.

"Oh, yes, I will take care of it."

Later Elly received another message from the shipping company. "Miss Hansen, we must have the money for your ticket immediately."

Again Elly called the secretary, and again she was told, "Oh, yes, I will take care of it."

Finally Elly telephoned the mission board director. "I have called this brother so many times to take care of the payment of my ticket on the boat. Why is it not done?"

After the director checked out Elly's complaint he was horrified to discover that the secretary of accounts had used up all the funds. "This is terrible, Elly. You were supposed to leave next week. But this man has confiscated all our funds. He has used all the money that belonged to the whole mission program. Everything! The money that was put away for the older pastors in the churches. Everything! What will you do, Elly? Do you still think you have a call to Thailand? Are you determined to go?"

A still small voice within assured Elly Hansen, and she answered firmly, "Yes, I still have a call to Thailand."

"Do you still believe that you are going?"

"I believe that the Lord can raise the money I need."

Two days later the director telephoned again, "Praise the Lord! We have all the money for your ticket."

What happened? Elly never learned the full details, but she felt that her firm faith inspired the director to telephone friends in churches all over Denmark. They rallied to her dilemma and raised not only her fare to Thailand but money for her living expenses in Thailand for a short time.

Elly contacted her parents about her trip to Thailand. Christian Hansen argued, "You're the oldest, Elly. You've got a good education as a nurse. You owe it to the family to stay here and help your family."

As much as Elly wanted her earthly father's blessing and good will, she desired far more her Heavenly Father's approval. "I will follow Jesus," was still her firm reply.

Carefully Elly packed a few supplies and personal effects in boxes. Still opposed to his daughter's decision, her father did not bid her farewell, but her mother did come to see her off. Elly took the train from Copenhagen to Hamburg, Germany, which was an eight-hour ride. Too proud to try to speak German, Elly spoke English and asked a policeman for a hotel connected with the East Asiatic Company. He hailed a taxi and sent her to the hotel, and from there she telephoned the company. "We are almost ready to go. We will send a taxi for you immediately." The captain had finished loading all his cargo of machinery and cars on the large four-deck ship and was ready to set sail for the Orient.

When Elly boarded the ship, she met a Swedish Pentecostal teacher, Martha Perrson, who was a little younger than Elly. The women enjoyed their journey from

Hamburg through the English Channel following somewhat the same route that Asiatic Company ships had
sailed since 1732 when the company was founded. On
through the Mediterranean they sailed until they came
to Alexandria, Egypt. It seemed to them that the com-
pact pressure of darkness began to weigh on them as they
progressed into the Red Sea. Here everything was outside Christianity.

About this time the large cargo ship lost its anchor
in a harbor. "Well, ladies, you believe in God, don't you?
Our anchor has gone down to the bottom of the sea, and
it might be lying just beside one of the Egyptian iron
chariots from the time when Moses crossed the Red Sea.
Well, I don't believe God will perform a miracle and bring
our anchor up. I think I'll have to use ordinary manpower
to bring that anchor off the bottom of the sea." Elly and
Martha were not amused by the captain's teasing.

Day after day, night after night, the two young
women declined to join in many worldly activities on the
ship. Some of the other passengers were almost offended by the stand the women took, so the long boat trip was
not all fun and games for young, unmarried Christian
women. Elly and Martha spent much time in prayer and
studying their Bibles, so they were not harassed too much.
In later years, however, Elly preferred to fly. The girl
who liked to take stairs two at a time did not want to daw-
dle away weeks on a ship anyway.

At last the big ship docked at an island called Si Chang
because the big boats could not go up to Bangkok at that
time. Martha and Elly, along with some personnel from
the embassy in Bangkok, boarded a much smaller boat
to sail into Bangkok. After years of preparation, Elly had
finally arrived in the land of her calling.

Chapter 6
· · · · · · · · · · · ·

New Challenges

Thailand lies to the west, north, and east of the Gulf of Siam, which is an arm of the South China Sea. On the southeast it is bounded by Cambodia; on the east and northeast by Laos; on the west, north, and northwest by Burma; on the southwest by the Andaman Sea, a part of the Indian Ocean; and on its southern extremity by Malaysia. Its greatest length is 1,024 miles; its greatest width, 485 miles.

Unlike every other country of Southeast Asia, Siam has never bowed to Western colonial rule. In 1939 the name Siam was changed to Thailand, meaning "land of the free."

Not too far from the equator, Thailand is the home of fifty million souls. Almost one in ten Thais lives in Bangkok. The Thai people are friendly and are wellknown for their smiles. They avoid confrontations or displays of anger. Strangers passing on the street smile at each other.

Jai yen yen, the Thais like to say, which literally means "cool, cool" or "keep your cool."

Buddism is the principal religion. Thailand has 365,000 Budhist temples—300 in Bangkok alone. The founder of the religion, Buddha, lived about 450 years before Jesus.

Martha and Elly stood on the deck as they sailed into Bangkok harbor. They soon discovered that, although modern Bangkok is one of the world's most fascinating cities, the westernization that tourists observe is but a very thin slice of the country.

The girls' eyes opened wide at the picturesque canals and agricultural scenes which lay within walking distance of modern hotels, the exotic trappings, the oriental splendor, the tinkle of temple bells, the abject poverty, the saffron-robed priests, and the unique oriental faces. There are so many children, Elly noticed. She later learned that children under fifteen account for more than forty-three percent of the total population.

Elly realized, God has not given us a garden of pleasure but a white harvest field. Thailand is a land where people are burdened down with fear, agony, and sickness—a land where people bow down to idols and seek fellowship with the spirit world. Lonely and lost, they wander thinking, Nobody cares for me. But Elly and Martha came to Thailand to spread the good news: "God so loved the world, that he gave his only begotten Son, that whosoever believeth on him should not perish, but have everlasting life."

Yes, thought Elly, and we will also try to make life here in Thailand a little easier for the sick and shut-ins.

The director of the Thai mission work was waiting

on the dock to welcome the young ladies. He took them by taxi through the clamorous streets to the American Bible Society House. Later Elly went to the immigration office to get a permanent visa. She readily obtained a visa at a cost of only fifty dollars. "To renew, you only have to pay ten dollars each year," the immigration agent instructed her.

After three or four days in hot, steamy Bangkok, the women went by train to the province of Tak. The trip took two days. They traveled in jungle all the way through the province of Phitsanuluk. Late in the first evening the two girls came to a small hotel of sorts. Tired from the long journey and the completely different culture, they were also a bit frightened. Early in the morning about four o'clock the director called, "Time to get up, ladies! The rice truck leaves at five o'clock. Your *compat* [Thai food] is ready."

Hastily Elly and Martha dressed; gathered their belongings; gulped down the compat made from meat, vegetables, rice, and an egg; and hurried out to the truck. "What sort of meat was that, Elly?" Elly asked no questions about the strange food. She just offered thanks and ate what was set before her.

"Here, you ladies can sit up front with the driver," said the director as he crawled in the back and perched himself on the rice sacks.

"Do you suppose we'll see monkeys, elephants, or tigers today?" Martha wondered.

"Just so it isn't snakes!" Elly responded.

At noon they stopped in the province of Sukhothai and met an American doctor's daughter who was doing leprosy work there. Elly was impressed with her first look

73

at the leprosy work. There had been no leprosy in Denmark since the Middle Ages. In fact Denmark was the first country in Europe to stamp out leprosy. But leprosy was a stark reality in Thailand.

About four in the afternoon they arrived at the mission station in Tak Province. "We didn't see a single monkey, much less a tiger!" As they drove up to the mission Elly recognized the red, winding road and the church with a cross on top. "This is the very place I saw in that vision," she rejoiced. God confirmed her faith in her call to Thailand.

The next day Elly began studying Thai. Her mother tongue was Danish. In elementary school she had studied other Scandinavian languages, plus German, French, and English. In nursing school she studied Latin and in Bible school Greek and Hebrew, but Thai was a new challenge. "It even has a different alphabet, but if we work hard maybe we can learn those sounds, Martha."

"But all those different tones! How will we ever learn all of them?"

The resident missionary's family consisted of three children, and three single missionary girls were in language study. As soon as they realized that Elly was a trained, experienced nurse, they called for her when anyone was sick.

Shortly after she arrived Elly was invited to help in the leprosy work. In February 1953 she attended the first leprosy conference, held in Khon Kaen in eastern Thailand near the Laotian border. There she met a Baptist doctor, Dr. Burcer, who taught the group how to treat leprosy patients medically and surgically. Elly learned to do simple surgery on the ears. "I learned to sew them up so they would look nice, and I also learned to do some kinds of smaller bone surgery." Her long years of nursing training paid off. As she examined the *main en griffe,* or claw hands on leprosy patients, she did what her skillful hands found to do.

Elly's involvement in nursing and leprosy work somewhat hindered her language study, but she developed her own approach. "I would just walk down the street, smile at people, sit on their porches, and try to get a conversation going. I would write new words down and bring them home with me, then write them down seven times until I could remember them. Then I would ask my teacher the meaning. The first sentence that I learned in Thai was, What is this? I also soon learned two common expressions: *Bhar bhra diaw gon,* which means 'just in a little while' and *may ben aray,* which means 'it doesn't matter.'"

Soon she chattered away in the everyday language of the common people to every Thai she met. From her classroom teacher she learned the religious and official language.

Hazel Hanna, an older missionary lady, realized that Elly was an energetic, enthusiastic person who was not willing to wait forever to learn all the particulars of the Thai language, so she began to take Elly out to a village every Sunday. They rode bicycles through the green, shady rain forest, and on the way she taught Elly a Bible verse. "Just say what I say, Elly."

"But what does it mean?"

"It's just a few words of a Bible verse, Elly. This will get you in touch with the people. Also let me teach you this little song." The Thai people particularly enjoyed the colorful flannelgraph stories. "We will use any kind of

means we can to get the gospel of Christ to these people," Hazel Hanna declared.

In this way Elly learned the Thai language from country folk. Her accent was not always considered classic
Thai.

In February 1953 Fern Burk, an American nurse,
received a telegram, "Come home immediately. Your
father is very ill." Fern was a competent nurse whose
father was a doctor.

"Elly, we need you to take care of the leprosy clinic
work." Elly inherited the challenge of taking charge of
the clinical work in three provinces—Tak, Sukothai, and
Kamphaeng Phet—and she stayed very busy.

Elly soon learned that Thai food differed greatly from
Danish food. The staple of the Thai diet was rice. "Is it
because flour gets weevils so soon in the tropics? I sure
miss those good Danish pastries." Every morning ox carts
rumbled into the towns, bringing fresh produce for the
market: ducks, chickens, pigs, and many kinds of delicious
fruits and vegetables. A dozen varieties of chili peppers
were displayed in the vegetable market, each represent-
ing a subtle gradation of heat, from so-called mild to
atomic. In the hot season, many different kinds of
mangoes were available.

The missionaries bought their fruits and vegetables
fresh every day because they did not own a refrigerator
at first. Eggplants were in abundant supply, so the cook
boiled eggplant with milk and cheese in the morning, then
stewed eggplant with a little bacon at the midday meal.
Bacon was very expensive. They had to drive sixty-five
kilometers to Nakhon Sawan for flour, bacon, bread, salt,
sugar, tea, coffee, butter, dried milk, margarine, kero-

sene, and soap. To give the faithful eggplant another face, the cook offered curried eggplant for supper. "Eggplant is the cheapest food available, dear." Other vegetables served were cauliflower, tomatoes, onions, and all kinds of peppers to spice up everything.

Elly was initiated to new kinds of Thai food early. For breakfast her first morning, a large, fat, oily fish (eyeballs and all) stared up from Elly's plate. "Well, this is not Danish ham and eggs, my girl. But you must learn to eat what is set before you." After fervent prayer she ate part of the fish—not the eyeballs—and she kept it down! "But when I get to know the cook a little bit better, I'll teach her the proper way to prepare fish," she promised herself. "I know how to cook seafood."

Five o'clock tea invariably consisted of bread, jam, and peanut butter, which was new to her Danish taste. Despite the sixty-five kilometer drive, the missionaries kept flour on hand after they got their kerosene refrigerator. Elly's strict training in London stood her in good stead, and she adapted to new food and different cuisine quickly.

The Thai people ate ants, termites, grasshoppers, lizards, frogs, and snakes. Elly discovered that flying white ants at just the right stage, when toasted, tasted almost like chestnuts. Another strange insect to Elly was available in August when the rains were heavy. The children gathered these and sold them for a good price. "They love them in Bangkok. You can get many *baht* [Thai currency] selling these insects in Bangkok. Toast them in warm ashes. Very good!" Occasionally the cook took the legs and wings off almost any hard insect, chopped them up fine, added lemon juice and white onion or garlic, then served the dish.

Bamboo shoots were a special delicacy. Elly soon made fast friends with the cook, who was very industrious. She encouraged all the people to collect bamboo shoots for her. "I will prepare them," she promised. She got an old gasoline tin that would hold twenty kilograms, cleaned it good, and used it for preserving the bamboo sprouts. "This will make good curry." Every year when the rains started the young people from the church went out to the jungle to collect bamboo sprouts. "These will be very good for Christmas!" the cook declared encouragingly.

Elly set up a schedule for working in the villages. The clinics were usually located in the homes of people who had leprosy. Ordinarily, leprosy patients kept to themselves. They could hardly believe that the tall, red-haired Danish girl was truly interested in them with their exposed bones, stubby feet, and misshaped hands and ears.

One father came to the clinic with swollen hands and broken skin. "No one cares about me," he muttered.

"For God so loved the world, that he gave his only begotten Son." Elly could think of no greater comfort for this hungry-hearted, desolate leper than John 3:16. She often quoted it as well as she could in her beginner's Thai.

"Can this be true? A God who loves me?" The leprous man was astounded at such great love. "I was in such misery, I could not stand it anymore. I had decided just to finish my life. I had found sixteen poison leaves and I was ready to say goodbye to all, walk into the jungle, and die! Now I am *not* going to die. Someone really loves me!" Later this man became a pastor in a leprosy village. He served faithfully until the Communists shot him. But the church still stands as a monument to the love of God shown through the ministering hands of a dedicated Danish nurse who was determined to follow Jesus.

Elly nursed by day and studied Thai by night. In six months she was reading her Bible in Thai.

The call for help came daily. With all the faith she had, Elly responded to every call, because her heart was hungry to know God more fully and to see Him at work.

One day an urgent request came. "Come pray! Kangaeb is insane. She has been foaming at the mouth and screaming day and night for a month. We have to chain her."

"Oh, Jesus, help me," Elly prayed. "I plead the blood. Let me be clean so the devil won't have a chance." She knew the woman was in the depths of despair and in the darkness of spirit worship. She carefully placed her Bible on the woman's head, then put her hand on the Bible. As she prayed the convulsions stopped and Kangaeb became quiet.

"Take off the chain," Elly instructed.

"No," answered Kangaeb's sister. "She has kicked water pots and broken glasses. We cannot turn her loose."

"You wanted me to pray; now believe! Give me the key," Elly commanded. From that day Kangaeb was free from the demons who had tormented her.

Later while Elly was lying in bed she was suddenly thrown out. About that time the other missionary girl came down the staircase saying, "I am so scared. I was thrown out of my bed!"

"Well, I wondered what I was doing on the floor," Elly responded. "I was thrown out of bed, too. Let's pray. I believe Satan did this because he is angry that Kangaeb has been delivered." Elly knew that the power of the devil was real.

Every Saturday Elly rode her bicycle seven miles to the village in Tak Province where the people with leprosy lived. From early morning until late in the afternoon she ministered not only by nursing but also by reading her Thai Bible and giving Bible lessons illustrated with flannelgraph. She carried her own food and drink.

Before long she noticed that one of the leaders of the Bornea Tea Company seemed concerned about her. This Englishman often waited at the gate of his compound with orange juice and something sweet.

"I'll walk up the hill with you, Miss Hansen," he began. Then he told her, "My grandfather started Sunday schools in England."

"Are you saved?" Elly asked

"What do you mean? I have always gone to church and Sunday school." The man invited Elly's director, Dr. Burcer, leader of all the leprosy work in Thailand, for Thanksgiving dinner. "And be sure to bring Miss Hansen and the other missionary lady with you, Dr. Burcer. We'll go for a ride on my river boat."

On the boat, the enterprising Englishman directed the other missionary lady and Dr. Burcer down the staircase while Elly was helping with the table. When she started to go down the stairs, he barred the way.

"No, you can't go by," he teased.

"Oh, yes, I am definitely going to pass by, and don't you touch me!"

"Oh, Elly, you must know how I feel about you. Will you marry me, Elly?"

"You know missionaries cannot marry during the first two years while they are on the field. But I'll think about it. Now let me go down." Elly only wanted to join her friends.

Later the Englishman took his case to Dr. Burcer.

"He really and truly wants to marry you, Elly," Dr. Burcer acknowledged.

"Well, I don't dislike him. He is a nice man and he seems to be a good man, but I don't have any feeling in my heart for him. He must take that for an answer. I did tell him I would think about it, so I'll let you give him the answer. I am not going to marry him. I feel that the Lord wants me to settle down in Tak and work with the leprosy people. I am going to follow Jesus."

Once again the longing to follow Jesus fully led Elly to renounce her personal happiness and commit herself wholly to God.

Amporn's son and Ping's daughter. Children under fifteen make up 43% of Thai population.

81

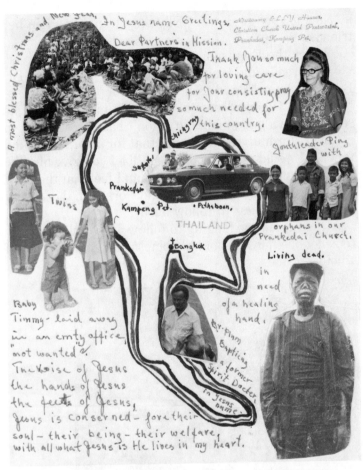

Newsletter from Elly Hansen. Note the leper in lower right corner.

Chapter 7
. . . .

A Refrigerator, a Land Rover and a Bathroom

After her initial training on the field, Elly faced the decision of where to locate permanently. Initially she planned to stay in Tak Province, because in many parts of the province just about every other house had someone with leprosy. This is where I am needed most; I am going to settle in this place, Elly decided. But it was not as easy to do as she thought.

"You can move to Chiang Mai, north of Phran Kratai," her supervisor advised. In 1954 there were about 100,000 people in the whole province. Chiang Mai, with its crumbling seven-hundred-year-old city walls and a moat full of red lotus blossoms, was a slumberous, quaint provincial town with a definite Burmese influence. It had a gentle, rather languid charm far different from that of Bangkok and its six million souls. It was famous for the beauty of its hand-painted parasols and the charm of its women. Beauty contests are extremely popular in Thailand, especially in the north. In the past, efforts have been made to exclude Chiang Mai girls from the contests because they win them far too often. The tall, reddish blonde Danish nurse made a striking contrast to the Thai ladies with their high cheekbones, ivory skin, and almond eyes.

As Elly settled in Chiang Mai and continued the leprosy work, she talked to the governor. He took her to a so-called health doctor in Phran Kratai for lunch. On the table were sixteen different kinds of food, but every plate was covered with flies. The streets of the town were mud and dirt and were often flooded. Only a few of the streets could be used by a car at that time.

The local judge and the governor both advised, "Stay in Phran Kratai and drive to Chiang Mai." But the road between the towns went through the jungle and hardly any one lived there. For twenty-four kilometers of the journey thick jungle prevailed. Bandits hid there, and danger lurked in the darkness.

Finally the authorities agreed that Elly could rent a house in Phran Kratai in Kamphaeng Phet Province. She and Martha moved there in February 1953. At first she rented the house of a leprosy family. "But we soon had to move again."

About the time that Elly moved, her director requested, "Elly, you must go up in the hills to get an elderly American missionary and bring her down here. She has malignant malaria, and it has affected her brain. She must go home. Poor dear, she came over here when China closed. She got her training as a girl at Wheaton and has been on the foreign field for many years with the Overseas Fellowship. She must be about sixty-five. She has been working in those hills with one of the tribes. We need a nurse to bring her down." The hill villages are often beyond the roads of civilization and the light of the gospel. The people live a hundred years back in time.

When Elly got to the missionary's station, she found a hopeless case. After Elly took care of her patient, she was offered the woman's big twelve-cubit-foot refrigerator at a very cheap price.

How will I get this refrigerator down from the mountain? Elly wondered. I will need four pairs of carriers to carry this heavy thing down the hill. With the help of good carriers she put ropes on the refrigerator and pushed a pole through the ropes. Once they got the refrigerator downhill they loaded it on a rice truck and took it to the river.

"We'll take it on the boat." So they sailed all the way down the Ping River, stopping almost in front of the mission house.

There more hired helpers pushed and shoved, but they could not get the big refrigerator through the door. "Let's just put it on the veranda. Get two big planks. You men are strong. Here is some stout rope. Just shoot it up on the veranda." Once the mission was accomplished they all rejoiced. "Now we can have cold drinks and keep our milk and eggs fresh."

"Could we make ice cream?" someone wondered. Refrigerators in the tropics are helpful indeed to make life a little more pleasant for overworked missionaries.

This was Elly's first appliance and she was very grateful.

Now that she had a refrigerator, Elly's next big problem was transportation. She prayed, "Lord, just help me to get an ox cart. My toes are infected from wading in this mud during the rainy season." The swaying, bouncing, lurching, jarring motion of an ox cart traveling down a winding muddy road appealed more and more to Elly as she lost her last toenail. The Lord in His wisdom sent not only an ox cart but also a fine gray Land Rover similar to the vehicle that the police in Thailand drive.

Dr. Burcer reported to the Danish church, "Elly needs a good Land Rover." In a short while funds were sent for the Land Rover and later for buffaloes and an ox cart as well. The leprosy people on the village farm need this buffalo and ox cart, Elly decided. I'll learn to drive the Land Rover.

For years Elly had ridden buses, trains, and bicycles or had walked to her clinics. Now at last she had wheels. With just four hours of practice Elly drove to the police station for her driver's license. The test was most simple: On which side of the road do you drive? When you pass a car on which side do you pass? (Perhaps this simple test explains today's traffic problem in Bangkok. Every person who wants to drive can pass the test!)

Dr. Burcer, who had delivered the gray Land Rover, said encouragingly, "Now, Elly, you are a licensed driver. Drive me home." All went well until they arrived at the gate of his house. "Whoa! Elly, you are too—oo close!"

Too late. Elly had already ripped off the gate.

"Let me drive, Elly. I learned to drive back home in Sweden. I already have a driver's license," Martha reminded Elly.

Martha proved to be a better driver, but Elly had places to go and things to do. After all, she had over a thousand leprosy patients in one town. "Now, I can really work for the Lord. I can carry the good news on wheels! Furthermore I like driving in Thailand. It's exciting!" She was right; driving in Thailand is very exciting!

One incident several years later was particularly amusing. On that occasion Elly drove a lady whose leprosy had affected her mentally from Phran Kratai to Chiang Mai, where the leprosy village was. Before she left Elly offered, "Here, take these two pairs of underwear. They will fit you. I want you to have them." At the last minute Elly also decided to take Tongbey, a baby she was taking care of. She put the baby in the front seat with her and the patient in the back seat, then cranked up the Land Rover.

Just before she left Martha came running out of the house. "Here, Elly, take this old monkey back up north and leave him. He's gotten to be a nuisance." Off Elly the new, inexperienced driver rode, with a black-eyed baby in the front seat, a mental patient in the back seat, and a monkey chained to the hood. Before they reached Chiang Mai they stopped for food. Her patient decided that she was not only hungry but also tired and dirty, so she found a spot near the river, took a bath, and washed her new underwear. When she came back to the car, she hung her underwear to dry on the back of the car, where it flapped in the wind. When Elly stopped in front of a shop to buy powdered milk for Tongbey, she spied the underwear. She calmly told the lady, "I think your clothes are dry now so just take them down." Off she drove again, ignoring the snickers and smiles of onlookers. That night as she related the story to the doctors and nurses at the leprosy colony, they laughed until the tears ran down their faces. "Monkey in front—underwear flapping behind—Elly, what a sight you must have been." Elly's sense of humor helped her handle the pressure and stress of her job.

When Elly first moved to Phran Kratai, there was not one bathroom in the whole town. "I know how to build a bathroom. I learned that in the Green Scouts." Elly drew up a plan on paper for the first bathroom in the town. "First we must dig a hole, then put in a floor, build walls, and attach a door."

"What do you need a door for?"

When Elly saw the bathroom the carpenters had built according to her plans, she burst out laughing. "For three months we used that bathroom without a door. Two people went together, and one would stand in front to be the door. Finally I saw a place that was making cement rings. Hah, I thought, now I can make a flush toilet. I told them to dig a hole two meters deep and two meters wide, put in the cement rings, fill up the side, and cement the floor. We used galvanized zinc plates for the walls and roof. There was no running water, so we got water from the well at the temple. I bought a clay pot that would hold about fifty liters of water." All the town came out to see that bathroom—the first bathroom in Phran Kratai!

"In the morning and again in the evening when it was not so steamy hot, the girl carried water for the kitchen and the bathroom in two containers hung on a pole across her shoulders. In Thailand many people go barefoot, so one always washes one's feet before going into a Thai house. Foot washing is common in Thailand."

Martha Perrson and Elly Hanson conducted leprosy clinics and Bible studies in this remote area miles from Bangkok. They were the first Christians in that area. Their medical supplies were furnished by the American Leprosy Mission, and Dr. Burcer supervised their work.

Eighty percent of the Thai people are farmers, and this area was farm land. About twelve percent of the population of Thailand are not ethnic Thai, and this number includes many tribal groups. The Chinese are by far the largest ethnic minority in Thailand, and most of the merchants are Chinese.

The village houses are made of teak taken from the thick jungles. The land lies between two mountain ranges, and the climate is hot and humid. Thailand is close to the equator, and during the hot season from the end of March through half of May, the temperature ranges from 100 to 120 degrees. Leprosy occurs most frequently in damp, tropical countries.

Thailand has three well-defined seasons: the hot season (March through April), the rainy season (May through October), and the cool season (November through February). In January there may be a "mango rain" which produces the mango flower. If this rain does not come, the fruit may spoil. A good mango year is very important. Mangoes and rice are the principle crops since the soil is very poor. "Dig half a meter and you will strike lava rock."

The rice fields are flooded because rice requires much water. The flooded fields are also used to raise fish. Fish, frogs, snails, eels, and snakes are all used for food. Cobras and other snakes are common and often invade houses and bathrooms.

Elly had over a thousand leprosy patients in her home area and saw up to eighty per day. She recalls that at the peak of her leprosy work, "I had over a thousand patients in one town, about seven hundred in another, and in the Tak we had about two hundred." She organized clinics in the homes of people with leprosy. She first determined the places that attracted the most patients, then announced, "A clinic will meet at this house." There were usually about two clinics per village.

Martha Perrson kept the records, carefully noting names and addresses and recording the medications. Elly used a sulfa drug in treatment as well as other kinds of medicine, including a large tablet of chaulmoogra oil. This was difficult to take so the patients welcomed diaminodiphenylsulfone (DDS) sulpha tablets, which were small. The treatment was dangerous to the nervous system, however, and if the patients got too much it disturbed them mentally. Occasionally small children got into their parents' medication, which sent them into convulsions and could cause death. Other patients developed allergies with painful rashes.

Each day Elly began every clinic with prayer and a Bible lesson, often illustrating the lesson with flannelgraph, flashcards, and homemade visual aids. Over and over she quoted John 3:16, but more importantly, she demonstrated the love of God to the Thai people.

Because they were leprosy patients these people were not too well accepted in their communities, and most of them had been sent to the far north to live.

The queen of Thailand had a wonderful attitude toward people with leprosy and was concerned that they be given the right to live a normal life. They were not completely isolated, but most of them did live far north, and this is where Elly chose to minister.

At the temples, however, lepers were never given status. They were not actually barred by the law but rather shunned by the people. They kept to themselves and usually lived in their own villages. Many withdrew from society because they were very poor and unable to work with their crippled hands. Many of them became beggars, and often their children were abandoned. Elly knew how devastating rejection was. She had studied psychology and knew how to minister to body, soul, and spirit.

In her desire and determination to serve, Elly boldly asked the mayor for farming land for people with leprosy. Many of these people came from farming background and had skills and experience in this area, but they needed land to farm. The mayor graciously gave two hundred and fifty *ray*. (One *ray* is about forty feet by forty feet, enough to supply rice for a family of three or four.) Elly set up a system to clear the jungle land which the mayor had given for farming. She moved ten families out to this project. Then she purchased water buffaloes, built two-wheeled wagons, and bought knives and axes to use for clearing the land. The first year she said, "I will furnish you with rice, garlic, and salt. The rest you must find in the jungle. You must plant vegetables, for you need vegetables for good nutrition. Get bamboo shoots; they will add to your diet."

In order to oversee the project herself, Elly had a small bamboo hut built, and she went out there to live alone. Martha tried to take turns with her, but she felt terribly scared and miserable. "She saw fireflies and thought they were tigers' eyes."

"You just stay here, Martha, and keep records. I will go live in the jungle," Elly decided. "I never see tigers, only wild pigs and snakes."

Often she had to wade through mud and water up to her waist. Leeches were a common pest. When the mud got under her toenails, infection set in, and Elly lost all her toenails several times. "When I was out there on the job, things went smoothly, but when the leprosy people did not have someone of authority to supervise there would be a big 'mouth fight' over the location of the well, the peanut field, the rice field and the vegetable garden. Leprosy people are very proud. Everybody wanted to be the head. No one wanted to be the hands and feet. All was confusion until I said, 'The well will be here. There is water here.'"

When they dug, sure enough, there was good water in the very spot where Elly had pointed. Slowly, meter by meter, the people with leprosy turned the jungle into fertile fields. How pleased they were when they had their very own farms.

Along with the farm land, a church was being formed. Pastor Boon Mak, a well-known Presbyterian minister from Bangkok, came and did the baptizing for Elly. As pastor, Elly performed marriages and conducted funerals, but she did not baptize in the river. Brother Boon Mak was highly respected because during the war with Japan (World War II) he had stayed true to Christianity. He, along with Brother Sook and Brother Bratsuk, had traveled and evangelized and kept the Christian faith alive when many turned back to Buddhism because of the danger and persecution. From the start of the work in

Phran Kratai, the mission was associated with Brother Boon Mak's church in Bangkok. Elly poured herself into this work, and after four years she returned to Denmark on furlough.

Feeding chickens to make money to help in the work of the Lord.

River baptismal scene in Thailand.

....

Chapter 8

A New Family

Elly arrived back home in Copenhagen about midnight one night in 1956. At three in the morning the doorbell rang. "Who could be at the door at this hour?" asked Elly's mother. When she opened the door she cried out, "Karl, what are you doing here?"

With twenty-four yellow tea roses in his hand Karl asked to see Elly.

"It's too late, Karl. Elly is tired from her long trip. She has been flying for more than eighteen hours. How did you know she was here? You can talk with her tomorrow."

Karl always kept in touch with Elly one way or another. Is he still in love with me? Elly wondered. Does he think I am home to stay? That I will not return to Thailand? Doesn't he know that I am determined to follow Jesus? My desires are strong for Jesus, and my life is dedicated to Him.

Tired though she was from four long weary years of nursing leprosy patients, there was not the slightest doubt in Elly's mind. It was good to see the Danish flag blowing in the breeze, to drive down Vesterbrogade, one of the busiest streets in Denmark, and to read the *Berling's Times* newspaper, but in a few weeks she began to worry about her leprosy patients. Before long she was flying back to Bangkok.

She returned as a full-fledged, experienced missionary. She was very aware of the challenges that awaited her, but she still hungered and thirsted for more of God—a deeper experience, a fuller revelation. "So much of my work in the gospel seemed stale and dry. Petty politics, strife, envy, and jealousy reared their ugly heads even among evangelical missionaries." But never once did Elly waver in her determination to follow Jesus. "Karl was nice. His roses were beautiful. It was good to see my family, especially my mother, but my leprosy patients needed me." She flew back to Bangkok, caught a bus north to Phran Kratai, and traveled further north to Chiang Mai.

Elly often rode the train before she got the gray Land Rover. Third-class trains in third-world countries make one pause three times before traveling. Every train is packed with people. Every door, every window oozes people. All the people are loaded down with luggage, and it is *not* Samsonite. In addition to bags and baskets of underwear and personal items, they also carry baskets of vegetables, chickens, cats, ducks, dogs, and piglets, not to mention numerous babies. Most third-world babies do not wear diapers either.

"Oh, Mrs. Taylor, and you were offended at the smell

of my Danish cheeses. God was just preparing me." But Elly rode third-class trains when necessary. Her energy, intense curiosity, and compassion for "her people" drove her on. Her innate sense of humor helped immensely.

Elly also endured some hair-raising experiences while riding buses. On one trip Elly was carrying a box of Gospels of John. That morning she put her money under the books, then put the box on top of the bus. That day bandits stopped the bus and ordered everyone off. For some unknown reason a man shoved Elly aside and stepped in front of her. The bandits killed that man immediately, then ordered all the others to lie face down on the ground while they searched through their luggage for valuables to steal. From time to time the bandits hit their victims in the back with their guns, warning them not to resist but to hand over rings, watches, and anything valuable. One cruel bandit struck a heavy blow to the back of Elly's neck. "O, Lord, help me!" Elly prayed as she suffered excruciating pain from the blow. A peace came, and she felt that God had heard her prayer. Other bandits hit her on the back, but at last the ordeal was over, and the bandits went roaring off through the jungle. "Thank you, Jesus," Elly breathed as she stumbled to her feet. "They did not get my Gospels or my money. I think I am all right." The cruel blows left their mark on her body, however.

Another time the bus driver had a premonition that there might be bandits in the area. He cautioned everyone to lie flat in the bus so that it would appear to be empty. Bandits were in the area and encircled the bus but then someone shouted, "It's empty!" so they ran back in the jungle to await other victims. Despite the danger, Elly continued to travel frequently through the countryside to minister and bring the good news.

When buses and trains were not available Elly occasionally rode on trucks. The departure time for trucks was often quite uncertain. One hour might pass and then two hours, but the answer to inquiries as to the estimated time of departure was always the same—"bhradiaw, bhradiaw," which means "in a little while." Elly often got up as early as five o'clock in the morning to ride a bus or a truck to another town. Then the vehicle might finally depart about nine o'clock. The passenger dared not leave his seat, however, lest another traveller take it.

When she traveled to various towns to hold clinics for the leprosy patients, Elly often had to look for a ride on a truck. "One time when I was returning from Sukhothai, I rode on a truck filled with pineapples. There was no place to sit except on the pineapples. Try to imagine what it is like to sit on pineapples. I can assure you that pineapples can be very annoying to sit on. They are hard and kind of pointed. I felt like I was sitting on open safety pins. It is a good thing that we do not wear stockings out in that country because they would not look nice after such a trip.

"Another time we had to sit among large bags of dead fish. Imagine that smell!

"When several people are traveling on a truck someone calls out to the driver, 'Stop, I have to get to a bathroom.' Perhaps you wonder, Where is the bathroom? The passenger just steps down out of the truck, beside one of the wheels.

"The first few times this occurs, you might be a little bashful at this kind of scenery, but after a time, you

get used to almost everything. In the end you simply ig-
nore almost everything. Otherwise you may go twelve
hours without seeing any private place."

By train, bus, or truck travel in Thailand has its
frustrations and problems.

In 1954 God led Elly into a new phase of ministry.
A leper, who had only his knees to walk on, and his wife,
who had hardly anything left of her hands, came into the
leprosy clinic. The wife was expecting a baby and asked
Elly to be her midwife. The couple knew that they could
not care for the baby girl who was born to them, so they
just disappeared, leaving the baby with Elly. Tongbey,
whose name means Little Golden Leaf, became the first
baby of forty-six children that Elly helped to raise. She
was already caring for eleven children whose parents were
lepers, but Tongbey was the first baby. Not all missionaries felt the deep compassion for the children whose
parents had leprosy as did Elly.

"We must find Christian homes for them, Elly. We
must find parents who will adopt them." The first eleven
children were placed in homes, but Elly continued to try
to help them and look after them.

When Tongbey was just past three she too was
adopted by one of the teachers. But Tongbey still
remembered Elly. "We were busy and didn't have time
to care for you, so Sister Elly took care of you for us,"
was the explanation given to the child.

Elly not only nursed and cared for her children, but
she was also very interested in their education. "My
parents did not help me get an education. I must help
these children," she said. She set aside money every
month from her meager funds to help educate the

children. During the six years of training that the children of the lepers received, they learned to read as well as to use their hands in a practical way. These children did not usually have leprosy, but their parents did.

Once while Elly was on a mission of mercy for a missionary wife who was very sick, she found another baby who needed her. The mission authorities had flown their patient to the Presbyterian hospital in Bangkok for an operation. Elly took turns nursing her after surgery. While she was there, a lady from the Christian Missionary Alliance brought her a little boy.

"We found him in a bush outside the leprosy colony here in Bangkok. Isn't he beautful? Can't you take care of him, Elly? You already have Tongbey."

"Well, what shall we call you? I know, we'll call you Moses, because we found you in a bush."

In June still another baby came under Elly's care. "This baby boy is Chinese. Let's name him Bunlert, but we'll call him Timmy. How bright and clever he is!" That made three babies for Elly to look after.

The Thai people were Elly's people. Although her father had rejected her when she decided to follow Jesus, yet the Lord gave her a family of "rejects" and she devoted herself to them. She comforted herself with this thought when she received word of her father's death in 1958.

Martha, Elly, Tongbey, Timmy, and Moses lived together in a rented house in Phran Kratai. The children had their health problems. Tongbey suffered from tuberculosis as well as from leprosy. Elly was a working mother. She fed, nursed, disciplined, and loved her family, always teaching and asking God for help. But diapers, colic, and crying babies were not the only trials Elly had.

Late one night Elly woke up. Why is that dog barking? she wondered. What is that queer noise? Where is my flashlight? Quietly she eased to the crude door, carrying with her a heavy iron bar. There she saw a long knife protruding through the door. She hurled the iron bar down so hard on the knife that she hurt her own hand. Then she quickly barred the door and shut it more firmly.

"What happened?" Martha whispered her eyes big as saucers.

"Go to sleep. I think I must have given that would-be robber a shock. I even hurt my own hand when I hit his knife," she grumbled. But the girl who had withstood German soldiers was not intimidated by Thai robbers. When action was called for, she acted.

The next morning Elly got a call. "Can you come help our father. He is very, very sick. He needs a shot. It's not far to our house. Please come."

Elly was always quick to respond to needs and went on her errand of mercy. "I must pray for you first," she instructed. First prayer, then medicine was her method of treatment.

Late that afternoon another Thai neighbor questioned Elly. "How is it that you go to that house? Don't you know that he tried to break into your house last night."

"No, I didn't know that, but it doesn't matter," Elly replied. Her practice of returning good for evil soon brought its own rich reward. As soon as the man got well he went fishing and caught a very big fish. "Here, Miss Hansen, I want you to have this fish." From then on he smiled and spoke to her and became a very good neighbor. There was no more robbing.

In 1960 a man named Chalore, also called Nai Ban, came out of his house to watch as several converts burned their spirit houses. These miniature houses are said to be the dwelling places of spirits. People pray and worship before them and place flowers, food, money, and other offerings in them. While Chalore stood watching the burning, Elly approached him and began to talk with him about Jesus.

"Oh, yes, I have heard some of your singing. I like music," he smiled.

Chalore's home town was a wicked place. Buffalo thieves were common and these thieves became killers if anyone got in their way. If someone wanted an enemy murdered, these killers would do it for one thousand dollars, but some said that tribal killers would kill for as little as ten dollars.

As Chalore grew up he became involved in robbing and later became a hired man hunter, a killer. He was clever, and to cover his atrocious activities he went to the temple and had the monks to say secret magical words over his amulets to protect him in his evil work.

Each year after the rice harvest when everybody was happy, Chalore enjoyed his music. His monk teacher in the spirit world joined him in playing music and drinking rice wine. Despite his lifestyle, Chalore somehow remembered his talk with Elly.

Chapter 9

Tuberculosis

Running several leprosy clinics, farming, and raising eleven orphans and three babies kept Elly busy for long hours every day. She often fasted on Saturday, and after her clinic work was over she took her Bible and tried to find a quiet spot to pray. She felt drained, and the dull, dry church services did little to revive her flagging spirits. She began to lose weight. Finally she got down to ninety pounds. When she began to spit up blood in the mornings, she knew that she must see a doctor.

She did not tell Martha about her problem. "I've got to go to Bangkok on business," she explained, knowing how scared and worried Martha would be if she told her about spitting up blood.

In August 1959 Elly saw a Danish doctor in Bangkok. He X-rayed her and took saliva samples. Later he showed her the X-rays.

"See this spot on your lung, Miss Hansen? It is as big

as your hand. Also look at this black spot. It looks like a big cavern or sore where the tissue has been eaten away. You are a nurse, Miss Hansen. You know what this means. You have tuberculosis, and you must return to Denmark immediately."

"Well, if I have to leave Thailand I must move out the right way. I have to get my permanent visa first so that I can get a new entrance visa when I return."

"You will never come back to Thailand, Miss Hansen. You had better just settle down and realize that," the doctor said firmly.

But that doctor did not know Elly Hansen. Desire, determination, and dedication ruled her life. She still had an inner hunger, a longing, to know even more of this Jesus whom she had followed so long. She felt that missionary service in Thailand was the best way to satisfy her hunger.

Elly went to see about the matter of the visa, for she was always careful to do nothing to jeopardize her residence status in Thailand.

The staff at the Danish embassy were very nice. They sent her in a car to take care of her affairs and radioed via East Asiatic ships to her mission board back in Denmark. "Put her in the Royal Hospital in Copenhagen. They have a TB ward there."

Before Elly left Thailand she sought out Brother Boon Mak, her Presbyterian minister friend, as well as Brother Chaiyong and Brother Sook. "I need prayer. I need healing," she explained. These faithful pastors anointed Elly and began to seek God earnestly. As they rebuked the sickness, Elly had a strong inner feeling in her heart that God had taken care of the tuberculosis. "A stream of something went through my body."

On Friday she flew to Copenhagen and was surprised to see an ambulance waiting for her at midnight when her airplane landed. One of the missionary board members met her. "You are to go directly to the hospital, Miss Hansen."

Still coughing, but with a lump in her throat and tears in her eyes, Elly was back home in Denmark again. "There's the green, green grass of home. And there's the flag."

Since it was a hot August night Elly immediately demanded, "I want a bath."

"You are deathly ill, Miss Hansen. You cannot have a bath," answered the nurse.

"I have been on that plane for so long, I am filthy. I want a bath before I see a doctor or anyone."

"Okay, take a bath then."

In Denmark dawn arrives about four o'clock in the morning in summertime. Elly had all her personal possessions—bags and all sorts of things—holed up in the small hospital room that she shared with a young girl. As soon as dawn broke Elly began to sort through her things. The nurse on duty heard the noise. "Will you please get yourself to bed and do it quickly. We cannot disturb this hospital at this time of day."

"It is light out there, sister. The birds are singing. What time is it anyway?"

"Are you crazy, girl? You are a nurse. You are supposed to have some sense. It is four o'clock in the morning. You get to bed right now!" Elly the nurse had a hard time becoming a passive patient, but she had met her match. This nurse was very much in charge and would stand for no nonsense.

"I thought it was seven o'clock in the morning because it is daytime," she tried to explain. "In Thailand the sun rises about six."

"Well, this is Denmark—not Thailand. I will take care of all of your luggage and everything. You just get to bed and *stay* there."

"Well, I just wanted to help with all my stuff. You have so many patients. . ." Elly was used to being the nurse in charge—not a patient.

Professor Wuarberg, the Jewish doctor whom Elly had helped hide from the Germans, served as chief-of-staff of the hospital. He was also life physician to the king of Denmark and one of the top men in medicine in the nation. The first thing he did was to order a complete set of X-rays—forty-eight pictures in all. At eight o'clock Elly was rolled into the X-ray room for the lengthy X-ray session.

They pumped up everything that was inside Elly's stomach then put a microscope down her lungs for further examination.

"Let's take a biopsy too." The biopsy required anesthesia. When Elly began to regain consciousness from the anesthesia, she began to speak in Thai.

"What are you saying? What are you saying?" Dr. Wuarberg asked.

Elly replied in English, translating what she had said in Thai and excusing herself for speaking in Thai. But the doctor still asked in Danish, "What are you saying? What are you saying?"

Finally Elly understood. "Danish! I must speak Danish. I am home!" By this time Professor Wuarberg, along with other doctors and nurses, came in with the X-rays. They rolled her bed into a corridor and put the new X-rays on a glass showcase alongside the X-rays that had been sent from Bangkok.

"What kind of a doctor did you see in Bangkok?" asked Professor Wuarberg. "Perhaps he has sent the wrong X-rays."

"No," replied Elly. "Those are my X-rays from Bangkok. Those with the large spots on my lungs. A Danish doctor took them."

"But there is no spot or cavern on these X-rays that we took today. There is not even a shadow. There are no tubercular germs in the material taken from your stomach, and nothing showed up in the biopsy either." Ten days later the doctor talked with Elly again. "We have refined the biopsy taken from your lungs, and there is nothing wrong anywhere. What has happened to you? You couldn't possibly be healed just because you flew from Bangkok to Copenhagen."

"Well, Dr. Wuarberg, between those two sets of X-rays, I had three evangelical pastors in Bangkok anoint me with oil and pray for me in the name of the Lord Jesus Christ."

The good Jewish doctor did not like the name of Jesus Christ, but Elly insisted, "If I am what you say I am, then God has healed me."

"Well, then," Dr. Wuarberg agreed, "Jehovah God does still work miracles as He did in the time of Moses. One other question, Miss Hansen. When did you break your neck?"

"Break my neck? What do you mean, Dr. Wuarberg?"

"See that crack in your neck? At some time, somewhere you have broken your neck, but it has healed perfectly."

Then Elly remembered the heavy blow when the bandit on the bus struck her on the neck. "Oh, Dr. Wuarberg, the Lord does heal!" And she told him of the great God who had saved her from the bandits and even healed her neck before she, a nurse, had realized that it was broken.

"Well, Jehovah God does indeed still work miracles. On Monday I want you to teach and preach to all my university medical students in the auditorium of our hospital."

Elly begged for pajamas in which to make her appearance before the medical students, but the nurse in charge snapped, "No, just the regular hospital shirt." Elly swallowed her pride, prayed for God to help her and prepared her message. On Monday morning the nurse rolled Elly's bed all the way down to the auditorium where two hundred medical students awaited her.

"Tell us about your work with the people with leprosy. How do you do it? How do you organize your clinics? What treatment do you use? What medication? What sort of records do you keep? How do you protect yourself? What about your work with the children? Do you have an orphanage? How do you protect the children whose parents have leprosy?"

Elly the nurse answered their questions then, she gave her testimony as to how she became a Christian.

"Have I met you before?" asked Dr. Wuarberg.

"Sure, I brought you coffee and breakfast when you were doing work in the small laboratory in the basement of the hospital where you hid from the Germans in Birkerod."

"I remember now! So we meet again. Here in my hospital you are free to go wherever you will, with anyone who wants to take you anywhere. Also I will tell the kitchen to prepare whatever you want to eat. I am going to rebuild your body back to normal size, then send you back to Thailand."

Elly's friend Karl contacted her again while she was in Denmark. He had maintained contact with the Hansen family. Karl asked Elly if she would object if he married her sister. "You have my blessing," Elly responded. They were married, and since Karl was well off financially, they became a real blessing to Elly and to her mother.

While Elly was in the hospital in Denmark, her Presbyterian minister friend, Pastor Boon Mak, stopped by Denmark to see her. "I am en route to the United States to see a friend. I am glad to see you are better. I'll see you again in Thailand when I return." While Brother Boon Mak was in Denmark, he preached in several churches, and Elly interpreted for him.

The mission board was not quite as agreeable and enthusiastic as Dr. Wuarberg about returning Elly to Thailand. "Elly, you weighed less than ninety pounds when you arrived in Denmark. You were so sick. Regardless of what has happened recently, you came home because you were deathly sick. You must be careful. Don't return to your heavy schedule in Thailand too soon." When Elly gained seventy pounds due to Dr. Wuarberg's excellent care, the board agreed that truly Elly had experienced a miracle in her body.

Finally at the end of July 1960 Elly flew back to Bangkok, but she was a bit unhappy. She weighed 168 pounds. "Too much! I am too big and heavy. I must get back to work in Thailand."

When Elly saw Brother Boon Mak after she returned to Thailand, she soon realized that he had also gained something on his trip, but it was not body weight. He was a new man—full of fresh zeal, vision, and power.

Elly, the nurse, enjoyed teaching. Here she used a homemade visual of an elephant to reinforce her teaching.

Chapter 10

Boon Mak Meets Billy Cole

The friend whom Brother Boon Mak had planned to see in the United States had moved, and he was unable to locate the man. But the friendly Presbyterian with the large church in Bangkok made a new friend in the United States. He met Billy Cole, a United Pentecostal preacher.

Brother Cole soon explained the way of the Lord more perfectly to Brother Boon Mak, including the oneness of God and Jesus Name baptism. Before long, Brother Cole baptized Brother Boon Mak in Jesus' name. He returned to Bangkok a new man with new power. Shortly after he returned and preached the great news of the Oneness of God, he baptized twenty-two persons in Jesus' name, including Chaiyong Wattanachant, a friend and independent evangelist who had been preaching for more than eight years.

In gratitude to Brother Cole for teaching him the truth of Jesus' name, Brother Boon Mak invited the Coles to visit him in Thailand. The Cole family sought God, then packed up and left for Thailand.

When the Coles arrived, Brother Boon Mak planned a conference and asked Brother Cole to speak. Elly, along with other missionaries and Dr. Burcer, met at the Missionary Alliance guest house.

When Brother Cole, his wife, and his daughter, Brenda, came into the meeting, Dr. Burcer whispered to Elly, "Look at that family there. They have just arrived in Thailand to do missionary work, and they are bringing in heretical teaching!"

"Well," Elly responded, "I believe in prayer, and I believe we could just pray them out. Besides, the size of that missionary tells me that he could very easily have a heart attack. He must surely have high blood pressure. He may just have a stroke and have to go back again if we pray and believe."

Every year Elly continued to take a group of people to Brother Boon Mak's conference where the Cole family were. His was one of the biggest evangelical churches in Bangkok, and the Cole family lived in Bangkok also. During one of the conferences where Brother Cole was the speaker, he gave Elly an English book on the Oneness of God. She took it somewhat reluctantly, but as always, the hunger in her heart led her to a deeper place in God.

For many years Elly had poured herself into Christian service—nursing the sick, caring for the dying, feeding the hungry, planning work for the poor leprosy families, caring for abandoned orphans, delivering bound ones from chains of darkness and demons, dealing with opium users. But her own heart was almost drained dry. The formal church services she attended were dull, dry, and dead. Occasionally on Saturday after her clinic work she spent the rest of the day fasting and praying.

The Coles worshiped differently. Brother Cole would say, "Raise your hands and praise the Lord!" Sister Cole worshiped fervently with joyous praises. In spite of herself Elly was interested—almost intrigued—but still innately cautious and reserved. "Well, that is nice for them, but I am not so sure that I am going to do that."

After church one day the people arranged matters so that Elly sat with the Cole family at the noon meal. "Here, Sister Hansen, study this other book on Oneness," Billy Cole said.

In a letter of June 17, 1963, to the United Pentecostal Church International, Brother Cole mentioned that he had suffered some health problems but that God had wonderfully healed him many times. He continued:

> The church here in Thailand is making good progress, for which we are praising God. We know that you will not stop praying for the Lord's work here in Thailand.
>
> Prospects are great, and we are expecting a general revival throughout the whole nation in many churches. . . .Twenty-eight members and two preachers have already received the Holy Ghost. . . .In our own fellowship over two hundred who have received the Holy Ghost and a little less than four hundred have been baptized in Jesus' name. There are approximately one thousand attending our churches on Sunday. A missionary

from Denmark only in our last conference left her mission and joined us and brought her work with her. Only this week, Achan Boon Mak visited her work for the purpose of baptizing the first converts in Phran Kratai ever to be baptized in Jesus' name.

For three years Elly studied the material Brother Cole kept giving her, including a book on Acts. Every July Elly went back to the conference, and each time the invitation to be baptized in Jesus' name was extended, but each time she said, "I don't think I should at this time."

The first time Brother Chaiyong heard the message, he went home and prayed. He heard from God: This is right; do it. He obeyed gladly. He remembered that as a child in an independent Sunday school he had heard about one God, so when he heard Brother Billy Cole preach this message, he obeyed it promptly and began to preach this scriptural truth. He became a strong advocate for this message and is now the superintendent of the United Pentecostal Church of Thailand.

Although Elly hungered for more of God she was thorough, cautious and careful. As she continued to study carefully, she began to see that the Oneness message is what the Bible teaches.

Her fellow missionaries warned her against going to the conference where Billy Cole preached. About this time Martha Perrson left to return to her home in Sweden.

The United Pentecostal Church of Thailand began to prosper. Early in 1965 Brother Oscar Vouga, foreign missionary director of the UPC, visited Thailand. Brother Cole described the trip:

On Monday, January 27, long before daylight, we were up and getting ready to leave on a six-day tour. Each day demanded at least eighteen hours as we drove over mountains, plains, broken bridges, through creeks and what have you. One day in order to [reach] the train to go back into the jungle, we had to travel 20½ hours. Brother Vouga was completely adjustable to every condition. He even slept on the floor of a Nipa house [house made with thatch from the Nipa palm]. In fact my only problem was that he was too adjustable and wanted to eat the native food also. It was a real thrill to hear the Word of God go forth. It seemed that every word was from God. . . .I am now superintendent and need to be in the center of the nation [Bangkok]. We are in need of another family of workers from home so very much. We are responsible for thirty million people.

As is so often the problem in the Christian church, the harvest in Thailand was white but the laborers were few.

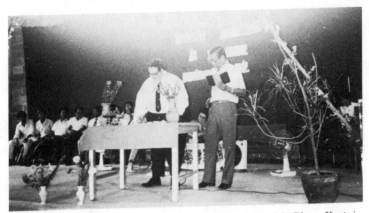

Brother Billy Cole and Brother Chaiyong in the new church in Phran Kratai.

Sister Chaiyong with Brother and Sister Billy Cole.

Chapter 11

Truth Triumphant

The week after Easter Sunday, at a camp belonging to Brother Boon Mak at Hua Hin on the Gulf of Siam, his church met for a conference. Hua Hin is about 250 kilometers south of Bangkok toward Malaysia. The villages strung out along the coast down the Gulf of Siam, an arm of the South China Sea, are almost exclusively devoted to fishing. This area boasts some of the world's most beautiful golden sand beaches, coral reefs, and deep water bays that teem with colorful fish and other sea life.

Many Christians from the north liked to attend these meetings, enjoying the services and also the sea. Although the Gulf of Siam is warm and tropical and very different from the Kattegat off the coast of Zealand in Denmark, Elly, who had grown up by the sea, thoroughly enjoyed her trips to Hua Hin.

The Thais have a passion for travel, especially by chartered bus with groups of friends. A group from central Thailand, for instance, will journey seven or eight hours through the night over perilous highways in order to arrive at the seaside resort of Hua Hin just before dawn. They will then have a quick picnic on the beach, watch the sun rise, and pile back on the bus for the long trip home.

Elly wanted to go to the 1965 camp because she felt so drained and dried out. I need a spiritual vacation, she admitted to herself. In the church or in her room she felt no liberty in the Holy Spirit. She was tempted to go out into the jungle to pray, but this was very dangerous for a woman alone. Bandits often hid in the jungle. Tigers and bears prowled there also as well as cobras. I'll enjoy the breeze and the sand and the sea at the camp, she thought. But a much greater joy awaited Elly at Hua Hin.

In her party were a Japanese Baptist pastor and two Thai schoolteachers. Right away Elly found work to do in the kitchen. There she met Pastor Frank Munsey from Hammond, Indiana. Elly later recalled, "We were sitting outside. They were having a business meeting which did not concern me, and since it was conducted in Thai, Brother Munsey was not interested in it either."

As they talked, Brother Munsey gently inquired, "Why don't you get baptized in Jesus' name, Sister Elly?" He relates, "I spent time the next three or four days explaining Pentecostal doctrine. On Thursday night we had a 'southern style' altar service. The power fell, and I began to speak in tongues in Thai. This convinced her that our experience was supernatural."

Finally Elly Hansen, realizing full well that the Bible did indeed teach this truth, was baptized on Friday, April 26, 1965, in the Gulf of Siam in the precious name of Jesus.

She walked out of the water speaking in tongues and walked up on the sand where Sister Cole waited for her, still speaking in tongues.

Elly remembers her experience vividly. "For three days and three nights the experience lasted. The sea was rolling, 'Hallelujah!' The wind was blowing, 'Hallelujah,' and the trees sang a Hallelujah chorus as they swayed in the Siam sea breeze." Day and night, day and night, Elly revelled in the glory of the Lord.

Other blessings fell. At that conference one of the older Thai women was healed. "She had been an invalid for twenty years. She could not even dress herself because of a stiff arm. As I was praying with her I told her, 'Just throw your hands up and give over to the Lord!' She did and the stiffness left her arm. It was completely normal."

"God gave me faith when I was seventeen, God was very real to me. I talked to Him and He answered me with an inner voice. Now I discovered that nothing is impossible in the name of Jesus!"

The meeting ended on a high note, and the smiling Thai saints went home rejoicing. The long trip wound back through the clamorous, glamorous streets of big, bewildering, sprawling, Bangkok with its teeming traffic of taxis, trucks, and jaunty little *samlohs* (three-wheeled vehicles), then up the highway that links the north with the south. All along the way the saints sang and rejoiced, but when Elly reached her mission station, the atmosphere was as stiff as the woman's arm had been. The mission authorities did *not* rejoice when they heard what had happened at Hua Hin.

Sister Elly and friends at Hua Hin.

Brother Frank Munsey preaches with Brother Chaiyong as interpreter. Note the handmade candelabra made by Ping.

Chapter 12

A New Church and a Miracle Baby

"Elly, we want you to meet the board concerning the affair in Hua Hin." All of the men and some of the women of the mission confronted Elly about her alleged involvement in heresy. The meeting lasted eleven hours, but Elly was well prepared for their questions.

"I did not go into this lightly. I have studied the Oneness of God for three years. It is truth. The Bible teaches it."

Question after question Elly answered confidently, correctly, and courageously, with no bitterness or hatred toward their hostility but rejoicing because her insatiable hunger for more of God was now completely satisfied. Her desire for God that had given her the courage to leave her father's home at seventeen years of age; her determination to follow Jesus and prepare herself to serve Him that had enabled her to work long, hard hours for many years to educate herself properly; and her years of dedication to the stress of dull, dry duty as a nurse on the mission field were now rewarded.

The waves of the sea rolled, "Hallelujah," the winds sang, "Hallelujah," and the trees swayed, "Hallelujah," but the board of Elly's mission work did not say, "Hallelujah!" She faced the cold, stony stare of rejection again. After one and a half months she was given an ultimatum. "You cannot stay here. You have no support. You cannot work with us because you believe heresy. Hand in the keys to the Land Rover. Someone else will take charge of all the leprosy clinics. You must go back to Denmark. No money can be used for you."

But Elly remembered when she was sent out from Denmark in 1952. The last word her board had said was, "Do not go by having faith in this board or the church or the people. Go by having faith in God." She also remembered the good teaching she had received at London Bible College. She remembered that when she had no money and when the school was closed for vacation with no place for her to go, God provided a castle in which to spend her vacation.

For three days Elly prayed and fasted. Then she told the board, "You did not call me to Thailand. God did. He helped provide for my nursing education. He found a castle for me to spend a vacation in. He will care for me now. I will not go back to Denmark."

Once again Elly left all to follow Jesus. Where to go? What to do? She was now a forty-one-year-old woman with many years of trusting God and leaning on Him. She was not seventeen, just beginning to walk with the Lord.

She was filled with the Holy Ghost and baptized in Jesus' name. She might go hungry for lack of rice, but she was filled with His goodness. The mission board and her fellow missionaries were not her only friends in Thailand. One of the Thai Christian families (not leprosy patients) had a house in the marketplace. When they heard about Elly Hansen's problem, they offered, "Open a clinic in our house in the market."

She turned in her keys to the Land Rover and the mission house, and left all the office equipment and records, as well as the refrigerator and other furnishings. Taking only her personal belongings, Elly Hansen moved to the marketplace to live very humbly and simply as did the Thai people. At first only the cook Tauwie followed her.

"I will go with you," promised Tauwie.

"I can't pay you anything. You had better stay here. I do not want to disturb your future."

"No, I go, too," said Tauwie firmly. She not only left with Elly, but she stayed with her eleven years. In addition to cooking, she also sewed most of Elly's clothes. Soon a little dog belonging to one of the mission men showed up at Elly's house in the market. Then other people began to come. The sick and the poor who are always with us needed Elly's nursing skills. Little by little, one by one, the smiling Thai people spread the news in the marketplace. "Come, see. She lives like us. If we have rice, we will share with her. She took care of all of our leprosy people for many years. Now we will take care of her."

Elly and the Thai people became mutually dependent, which is essential for true friendship. She depended on them for food, shelter, and clothing. They learned to look to her for nursing and spiritual leadership.

As Elly had done for many years, she first prayed for her patients before treating them. Soon she started a Saturday Bible school and later services on Sunday morning. On Sunday afternoon she sent out workers two by two to witness about God's amazing grace. Now Elly's ministry had a new fire, a special zeal, and a blessed anointing.

One night shortly before this time Elly heard a knock on the door. "Can you come, Sister Elly? Ban has been in labor for three days, but her baby has not yet been born. Can you help?" Ban was the wife of Chalore, who had talked with Elly when the spirit houses were burned down several years before.

Elly and several believers hurried to the home. When they reached the house the first thing Elly saw was a shelf built up as a spirit worship altar. It contained burning candles, sticks, a little plate of rice, two raw eggs, salt, money, and flowers, and knotted strings and holy water from the temple. A midwife was there, but the birth had become very difficult and complicated. The spirit doctor was also operating there. The dark danger of the occult and black magic pressed in upon Elly. There was much bowing and ceremony. Only Ma Sahmorn, Ban's mother, sat with folded hands and talked to Jesus. Elly surveyed the scene, then turned and said, "This will all have to be removed. Whatever I am to do must be done in the name of Jesus. I am not going to have anything to do with the spirit doctor or that shelf or the spirit worship. It all has to be removed."

"You are asking for trouble," the spirit woman

warned. Somjr, Ban's sister, was also very annoyed. "This baby has been on its way for three days and three nights. It is likely that the baby will die."

"I am here to help so that the spirit will not take the baby, and now you are going to take the spirit worship out of the place. You are asking for trouble," the spirit woman insisted.

Elly took out her stethoscope and examined Ban and saw that there was trouble all right. "My heart cried out to God in fervent prayer because the unborn baby's heart had stopped beating. But a still, small voice told me to believe: Just trust Me. I am going to show them just who God really is."

The spirit woman demanded, "The spirit told me that you should move the patient away from the window because this ground belongs to the spirits of this town."

Again Elly prayed fervently, "Lord, manifest Yourself in such a way that these folks will know Your power." She knew that defeat would mean the end of the influence of the Pentecostal church.

The people believed that the spirits of the dead lingered near when a new baby was born, so they used many enchantments to repel the spirits of the dead and protect the baby. Spirit retaliation meant mishaps: the babies stillborn or deformed. Now it looked as if Ban's baby would die. "God help us. Show us Your power."

"She needs to be moved away from the window," the spirit woman insisted. Spirit worship is always a desperate race to appease offended spirits before they have worked out their full plans.

"She is *not* to be moved," said Elly authoritatively.

Finally the baby was born—dead! Twenty-six friends

and relatives were in the room, and they all saw that the baby was dead.

"Pack up your bag but don't cut the cord," said the old people.

"Cut the cord," Elly demanded. Finally one of the women cut the cord. Elly then took the baby in her arms and began to pray.

Everyone was talking about the dead baby. "His spirit may come back and take his mother's life, too." Spirit doctors live in fear of retribution for unfulfilled promises, false claims, and lies that they have made to the spirits. The battle between the forces of good and evil raged on that night.

For forty-five minutes Elly prayed for the dead baby and the unconscious mother. Suddenly the baby began to get color, and he gave a little sound.

"Keep praying!" Elly commanded.

The baby gave a loud cry. As Elly continued to massage the baby's heart, his color and breathing gradually became normal.

Prior to this, Somjr and her mother had already decided to follow Jesus, but the baby's father was a bandit and a hired killer. He came into the room as Elly continued to pray for his wife. When the mother regained consciousness, Elly turned to the husband. "This baby was born dead. All your relatives saw that he was born dead. God told me that He was going to show that He is God. Now this boy has his life back. You do not belong to Jesus. You have not repented. To whom do you think this child belongs?"

"He really belongs to Jesus," the father of the child answered.

"Well, you are to take care of the baby. Should this child who belongs to Jesus have a father who does not belong to Jesus? Would this be right?"

"No! I want Jesus in my life now." He knelt down and prayed the sinner's prayer of repentance. Eventually, another new baby was born—born into the kingdom of God!

Little did Chalore know what the new birth really meant that night, but he began to grow in understanding. For two years he made only slight progress as he often traveled far away from the church to play with musical groups. At first he understood so little of the true meaning of salvation that he thought to receive Jesus was just to be owned by a superpower. When he was contacted again to be a hired killer, he called on Jesus to help him with his work. He could not understand why his shots went astray!

He became more and more interested in his music. He made a beautiful xylophone by hand and carefully tuned each note. He continued to study the Bible with Elly and the other workers. Eventually he and his wife opened their home for a meeting there. For almost eight years he was faithful to the work of God and served as a leader, but then came the time when he was overcome and slipped back into his old ways.

Elly earnestly prayed for and worked with her converts. She faithfully taught them the Word of God, helped them with their physical needs as a nurse, and helped them to find employment, but just as the rich young ruler went away sorrowfully because he did not want to pay the price for following Jesus so some of Elly's converts returned to their old ways. As said of Jesus in John 6:66,

"Many of his disciples went back, and walked no more with him." The loss of "children" was a great sorrow to Elly. She overcame these disappointments, however, and pressed on to greater victories.

Elly, Ping, and Sister Frank Munsey add music to a Thai service.

Pentecostals in America and Thailand enjoy food and fellowship.

Chapter 13
. . . .

Plum and Ping Accept the Lord

Buddhism is the religion of over ninety-five percent of Thais, reflected in 27,000 *wats* (major temples or monastery complexes) scattered throughout the country. In addition there are also 2,000 Muslim mosques, mostly in the south, and a number of Chinese shrines and Hindu temples, mostly in Bangkok. Christians, including Catholics, are said to be only one-half percent of the population, although some Christian leaders think this figure is definitely underestimated.

Almost every Thai male, from the king to the poorest farmer, regards it as a duty to enter the priesthood at some point in his life. Traditionally this is for one rainy season, between planting and harvesting, and often for a short two- or three-week stay during vacation as well.

Somjr's brother, Plum, was one of the Thai men who

had been a Buddhist priest. Then he saw the miracle of his little newborn grandnephew brought back to life. That evening Plum went to Elly's house with a question. "I saw God bring life back into my little nephew's body. Could He heal my malaria?"

Plum had suffered for some time with malignant malaria. At times he would lose consciousness. At other times he would go wild with the fever—go into delirium. Could he be healed? He had the desire.

Elly called some of the saints. They laid hands on Plum and began to pray, and he was delivered from malignant malaria. Occasionally he would have a light chill but never a severe spell in which he would lose consciousness.

Elly had not been surprised at Plum's request. About two weeks earlier she had seen a vision. "I saw him traveling toward a bright light. He was riding on a white horse, going up and up. He was on some kind of business. Very important."

The inner voice that often spoke to Elly told her, "This man has a desire to believe in Jesus Christ."

Plum, a very good mechanic, often helped Elly when she had car trouble. She would call to him, "Can you come over and see what is the matter with my Jeep?" Plum would cleverly locate the trouble and repair it. One day as he was lying down underneath the Jeep, Elly noticed a golden chain around his neck with numerous idols of Buddha hanging from the chain. Elly asked "Uncle Plum, God has told me that you have begun to seek for the light. Why are you still wearing that chain of idols?"

"How do you know?" Plum told Elly that shortly before this he had talked to Jesus and said, "If this woman is a godly woman whom You have chosen to do Your work, let her know that my heart's desire is to find the Savior." Then he declared, "Now I know that Jesus is God because He has done what I asked Him to do. You have fulfilled my request when you asked why I wear this chain." He took the chain off right then and never put it on again. He began to read the Bible with Elly each day.

Plum told Elly, "I was in the Buddhist priesthood for about four years. A lot of the Old Testament is like what the Buddhist priests teach. Buddha said, 'Seek until you find the One.' Now I have found Him. His name is Jesus."

Plum rejoiced. He had found what Buddha only sought for. Later Plum was ordained as a Pentecostal pastor. He now serves on the general board of the Thai church and also as secretary to Brother Chaiyong, the superintendent of the Thai church, which was nationalized after Brother Cole left.

The bringing back to life of the baby had still further effects. The baby's grandmother was an old lady who had been sick for some time with tuberculosis. She had one arm which was stiff in the joints, and she was unable to dress herself. Her children had helped her for the past twenty years. After the baby was healed the grandmother came to church for the first time. Later Elly called at her village because she heard that the woman was bleeding from her lungs. "I brought her to the hospital in the Jeep, because she was hemorrhaging. But the doctor simply said, 'She is not going to live anyway, so you can just as well take her home to her village. We cannot take her in here. She is contagious, and too many people from this hospital are dying. She is not likely to survive.'"

Elly did not accept that answer but asked if she could have some salt water. "Anything that will help her. I am going to take her all the way to the Overseas Missionary Alliance Hospital in Manorom." Elly and the saints prayed for the grandmother, and in spite of what the doctors in Kamphaeng Phet said, the woman survived. Her tubercular arm was healed when Elly was baptized at Hua Hin. Elly did not actually pray for the woman's healing but only that God would bless her and give her the Holy Ghost. Indeed He did give her a double portion and unlocked the stiff arm.

This family is name was Pornklar, and they had been involved in the work of bandits. Banditry and crime are serious problems in Thailand. According to the October 1982 *National Geographic* two to three dozen homicides are reported monthly in Bangkok, and homeowners dare not leave their houses empty for fear of burglars. A hit man can be hired for less than a thousand dollars per murder. Why is there so much crime? "Jade and rubies come from inside Burma," said one taxi driver. "And money for arms." Thailand contains the major supply line for the thirty-three-year-long civil war still being waged by the Karen people against the central government of Burma. Border areas and booty are up for grabs. Also eleven million people still earn less than two hundred dollars per year, which is considered the poverty level. Then the opium traffic is also a big factor in the crime problem.

The Pornklar family had been involved in this type of activity. They had been robbers and killers. Ping was a younger boy, about fourteen, in the family. As a small boy he thought it was great sport to steal chickens and ducks and whatever he could from the neighbors. Finally he was in so much trouble with the police that he just ran off to Bangkok, straight into the slums.

During the rainy season of August 1965 Elly and Plum drove down to Bangkok to try to find Ping. "I'll just take him into my orphanage if we can find him," Elly planned. Finally they found him in a galvanized-metal, ramshackle gambling place of the worst sort with drinking, street girls, and all other sorts of wickedness. They got him into the car and drove back to Phran Kratai. "You can be my helper, my watchman, Ping. I need some help in the house," Elly wanted to help the young man find some sort of direction for his life. At that time Ping had not repented. He still smoked, but not in Elly's house, and drank a little, but not openly.

Elly began teaching a class and started with Genesis 1. "God created man in his own image, in the image of God created he him." That's me, thought Ping. I was made in His image. Suddenly he understood how marvelous it is to be made in the image of God and how wicked it is to corrupt that image. He stopped smoking from that very day, and shortly after that he was baptized in Jesus' name. At a meeting in Bangkok Ping was gloriously filled with the Holy Ghost.

Elly, the former barmaid, had seen her own father drink. She herself used to light up a cigarette for breakfast, so she was moved with compassion to try to salvage a young life.

Her faith and her works have paid off. Ping has been a faithful helper for many years now. He became a serious Bible student and a reliable watchman.

Elly made a dear friend of a wealthy woman from Bangkok whose name was Gulab, which means *rose*. Mr. and Mrs. Gulab owned a jewelry shop in Bangkok. Her husband was a Catholic, but his wife persuaded him to tithe and give offerings. "God will bless our business if we tithe." The Lord did bless them, so Mrs. Gulab contributed money to Elly for a nice Jeep to replace the Land Rover she had left at the mission.

"Ping, I want you to be my driver," Elly decided, so Ping added chauffering to his other skills. Later, trying to develop some sort of work for her helpers, Elly set up a woodworking shop. Ping soon became a skilled woodworker and designed and built a beautiful seven-branched wood candelabrum for the church.

Elly also taught the Thai people to sing and make music. "Thai people are inclined to chant, but I taught them to sing hymns. I taught Ping to play my guitar. He soon surpassed my musical ability, so I turned it over to him. He is so clever now that I don't try to play anymore. He now teaches music to the young people, and he is in charge of the singing."

What a change was made in the Pornklar family! Robbers and killers became musicians and preachers. Delivered from tuberculosis and other sicknesses, they found life and health through Jesus Christ. Desire, determination, and dedication helped Elly to turn this family around.

Meeting Elly brought new life and opportunity to another small family in the jungle. Elly and some workers were driving a Toyota pickup truck through the jungle on their way to doing more evangelistic work when suddenly they saw a little hut. As they drew closer, they saw a man in the hut. "That man looks sick. We had better stop and see if we can help," Elly decided. After examining the man Elly said, "He looks like he has TB." With the man was his small daughter about ten years old. The child only had a small dirty rag tied around her waist-line—nothing more. For a living the man had been burning wood to make charcoal when he became sick.

"Help me put this man in the car. We'll take him back to the church grounds." At that time Elly had bought a nice plot of ground for the Phran Kratai church with $750 that Mrs. Gulab had given her. "I will take care of him, and if he gets better he can be a watchman over our church building as we build it."

When they got the patient on location, Ping and some other workers built a small bamboo hut for the man, but Elly took the little girl to her house in the marketplace. When she took the man to a doctor he diagnosed, "Double TB, hopelessly sick."

"Well, then, we must do what we can for him," Elly asserted. "First we will pray." After prayer the man did improve for some time. He was baptized in the Jesus' name, and when Brother J. C. Cole visited Thailand he received the Holy Ghost.

The little girl's name was Boonchuay, but Elly announced, "We'll call her Chu for short." Chu was also baptized and received the Holy Ghost. Elly questioned Chu, "What grade are you in? Where did you go to school?"

"I haven't ever been to school. My father and I have always lived in the jungle. He burned charcoal."

"Well, we must send you to school. I will go to see the head of education." Although there was some question, the authorities decided that Chu could start the first grade. She learned to read in one month and finished first and second grades in one year. She also learned to play the guitar and to sing.

When some of the people from Brother Boon Mak's

135

church came to visit they observed, "What a smart, intelligent girl! We would like for her to come down to Bangkok to our school."

Always eager for her "children" to have the best opportunities, Elly encouraged Chu to go. "You can help a family with their housework to earn your board. It may not be easy, as they have three children and there will be lots of housework and laundry, but you can get a good education if you work hard." The little girl from the jungle went to the big city of Bangkok and on to her third year of high school there.

Later Brother Chaiyong got her into another school and she came to live with his family. She has continued to pursue a higher education at a university. Once again Elly's loving ministry transformed a life both physically and spiritually.

Sister Chaiyong, Brenda Cole and Mrs. Gulab (Rose), who has contributed generously to the work in Thailand.

Chapter 14
....

Amporn and Ampai – a Double Blessing

On February 21, 1962, a Chinese man came seeking Elly. "The doctors in Kamphaeng Phet sent me to you. My wife died in the hospital there while giving birth to a child. The doctors say you know how to care for children. Will you take my baby? I cannot care for it."

"Well," Elly answered, "I will have to pray about that. You go down to the coffee shop for about an hour, and when you come back, I think I may be able to give you an answer." He did so, and Elly took out a devotional book that she was reading and began to meditate and pray. Soon she heard an inner voice: Take this child and feed it for Me.

"Yes, Lord, I will do what I can."

"I was living in the marketplace, studying the Oneness doctrine and somewhat lonely," she recalled.

When the man came back, Elly said, "I have prayed to God about the matter, and it seems I have an okay on it. You can bring the child." Elly had cared for other children before, but this was different. Living alone in the market, she received no regular support from anyone. "But the main thing this child needs is loving care, and I can give that." Elly knew the devastating effects of rejection on a child.

Elly received a grand surprise when the Chinese man informed her, "There are two—twin girls, born prematurely, and we cannot keep life in them. They need the kind of feeding which you have given to twins that you have cared for before." Altogether Elly had raised four sets of twins. But this tiny pair of preemies was a different sort of challenge.

When the man got off the bus with the twins in a little basket, the Thai people were smiling but their smiles were cautious and curious. One of the girls in her house questioned, "Are you going to take care of spirits? They are more dead than alive."

"They are not going to make it," predicted another.

"You are asking for trouble."

"They are no more than spirits. There's very little life in them."

"Nobody would take care of that kind of children," the cook protested.

Not a single "Barnabas" in all of Elly's group of workers tried to encourage her.

"I will have to encourage myself in the Lord just as David did," Elly declared firmly as she lifted the tiny doll-sized infants from the basket.

The smaller one weighed just two pounds, and the

other weighed only a little more. Their tiny heads were about the size of Elly's fist. Their arms and legs were like matchsticks. They had no eyebrows or nails, and they could not suck. Their body temperature fluctuated wildly. When it was hot their temperature shot up sky high. When it was a little chilly, down dropped the temperature until the babies went into convulsions.

Elly Hansen knew what it was to be rejected, and she responded to the challenge. She had the desire and the determination to save those two little scraps of humanity, and she also had her nursing skills.

"First I must bathe them. They are so dirty. Look at those blisters." She calmly began to treat large sores that were on the tiny bodies. Carefully she prepared a very weak formula—more water than milk. "I must not get their digestive systems upset." Slowly the twins learned how to suck and take nourishment.

When they were three months old, they weighed six pounds each. At that time Elly decided to take the girls, whom she had named Amporn and Ampai, down to Bangkok to see Brother and Sister Cole. Tauwie, the cook, went along to help.

After Elly's success with Amporn and Ampai, someone brought another set of twins to her. She kept them for a while but sent them back to their parents after they got strong enough.

Another child whom Elly raised was almost a twin: he was born ten months after his brother. The mother thought she could raise the first boy but she did not have enough milk for two. The mother attended church, and she kept requesting, "Pray for my baby. He screams all the time." The baby screamed because he was hungry.

To stop the screaming the woman gave the tiny baby opium ashes, after which he slept for three days and nights. Next she tried to feed him rice water—not very digestible for a tiny infant.

The people in the village told the local pastor about the case. He decided, "Sister Elly will take care of this baby. Sister Elly can work miracles with sick babies." The pastor brought the dying infant to Elly.

"I have a parcel for you," he said to Elly, handing her a small, ragged bundle.

When she opened the parcel the tiny two-week-old baby stared up at her. Elly's heart was touched by the child's desperate need. "I'll name this one Sandi. Sandi, I am going to adopt you." So Elly adopted the twins Amporn and Ampai and also Sandi.

Sandi's father had been murdered, so his mother thanked Elly sincerely for taking the child. "I cannot take care of him myself," she acknowledged. Although she still attends church she has never tried to interfere with Sandi.

Because Elly wanted her children to have good educations, she sent them to Brother Boon Mak's school in Bangkok for a while. Sandi later attended high school, then went to a technical school. "No one helped me with my education. I know how important a good education is in one's life so I want to help my children," Elly explained. She tried to set a good example for the saints in her church. "It is not enough to bring children into the world. One must be responsible for body, soul, and spirit. Our children must grow just as Jesus grew in favor with God and man—physically, mentally, socially, and most of all, spiritually."

Chapter 15
. . . .

The Burning of
Phran Kratai

One night in November 1966 about 8:00 p.m. Elly put the children to bed. The twins were small—about four years old. Sandi was less than a year old. Chu, from the jungle, was in kindergarten. While standing in front of her house, Elly suddenly saw a fire about one hundred meters away. "What is that? An explosion?" The fire began in the rice, then blazed out of control. Later the police suspected that someone might have set the fire using kerosene oil or gasoline. The fire burned rapidly into a rice mill, then caught another rice mill across the street. House after house burst into flames. "What can we do? There is no water and only one fire engine!"

"Send messengers through the jungle for help!" Elly thought, Oh, how I wish we had a telephone! Many towns and villages have no telephone or perhaps only one located

141

in the post office. When a call comes in, the person wanted must be located and then call back.

Before help could arrive almost all the homes in Phran Kratai had burned to the ground. Three rice mills were completely burned down, and four others were half burned.

Quickly Elly got the children into the World War II Jeep that Mrs. Gulab (Rose) had provided for her. Calmly she reassured the children, "Don't be afraid. Pray to Jesus." Ping took the children out to the church land which Elly had bought with money from Mrs. Gulab. Ping and other workers had cleared this land, and Elly planned to build a church on it.

When Ping returned, he and Elly worked quickly to get out their mattresses and what clothing they could. "I'll put the Singer sewing machine and our chairs in the water hole behind the house." Darkness hindered, but Elly worked steadily on by candlelight. She packed and carried furniture to the street, praying fervently all the while. Fire blazed for hours that seemed to stretch on and on. Scorching winds whipped the flames higher and higher. Shocked, the people watched as the uncontrollable fire sent yet another row of houses into a towering inferno. The roaring fire drew closer. Ping and his family kept praying, "God send a helpful wind." About 3:00 a.m. the police came and reassured them, "Don't worry. The fire is going another way. Go and check on the children." The rushing fire had abruptly changed its course and veered around. It raced away, leaving a train of smouldering houses. Burning red sparks speckled the black tropical sky. The last fluttering flames flickered out, but the hot ashes still occasionally flared up before they finally simmered down.

When Elly drove out to the church property, Chu and two neighbors were very excited. "A circle of angels stood around about us. Brother Ping prayed, 'Lord, spare this place.' Then God sent angels to protect us!"

Only a few china cups were broken and one mattress was lost. Usually many people steal during disasters like this, but as the children testified, "God sent angels to come and protect us."

Two boys in the town burned to death in their houses. Over one hundred homes burned. Many people lost all they had.

The next day the people tried to sort everything out. "One family was devastated. This was their third fire, and they had also suffered one robbery. The father threatened to commit suicide, so his wife came to me for help," Elly recalled. The calm, compassionate, caring Danish nurse had won the confidence and good will of the townspeople.

"I had six Chinese friends who were merchants. They were very generous. After this fire a new law was passed. No more wooden houses. All houses must have galvanized zinc roofs. There must be no gas or oil stoves in shops. All houses must now be built of brick."

There is always a silver lining to every cloud. After the burning of Phran Kratai, the city fathers improved electrical service from the River Ping. "Now we could have microphones and electricity, a P.A. system. Best of all now we could have running water and could use running water for a flush toilet." Elly began to dream of a large brick church in Phran Kratai, but she still had no support except a few gifts from friends like Mrs. Gulab.

Nevertheless Elly began to dedicate herself to this dream.

Later Elly erected a simple building of bamboo poles and leaves for shade on the land which she had bought with the $750 gift from Mrs. Gulab. Here Brother Oscar Vouga and Brother Billy Cole visited her.

"We just had chairs for Brother Vouga, Brother Cole, and me. All the others sat on the grass. I suppose Brother Vouga was shocked at the simplicity and poverty of our efforts."

Sister Vouga stayed in Bangkok with Sister Cole in the Cole's home. She recalls showering in a tank bath. "Just a tank up high, and I sorta sponged off. When Brother Cole and Brother Vouga returned from Phran Kratai they were covered with mud from head to toe. The roads were terrible—just red ooze. The tank bath really got a workout from those two. All they said was, 'We ran into some bad roads.' " Brother Vouga and Brother Cole gladly drove long miles in order to spread the gospel and encourage Sister Elly.

About this time, almost twenty-five years after World War II was over, Elly was surprised to find that she still had some bitterness toward the German people. A German businessman lost his way in northern Thailand in the province of Kamphaeng Phet, and he stumbled into the police station.

Not proficient in the Thai language, the man spoke first in German. When he found out that he was not communicating, he tried English.

"Ah, ah, you speak English. You need to talk with Miss Hansen," said the policeman. He directed the man to Elly's house.

"A German? Way up here in Phran Kratai!" Elly had

to pray earnestly before she got control over her anti-German feelings. She did pray very effectively, however. As in the case of Corrie ten Boom, God's love filled Elly's heart for her former enemy. There is no pit so deep that His love is not deeper still, she thought. Jesus died for this man just as He died for me! She began to witness to the German man so lost in more than one way and so far from home. On and on they talked about God and the wonderful truth of the gospel. About one o'clock the next morning, Elly convinced him of the truth.

"Hurry, Pastor!" She called the local Thai minister. "This man wants to be baptized in Jesus' name!" For several years Elly kept in contact with him after he went back to Germany as a teacher.

Chu, the girl from the jungle, and Ampai, one of the twins whom Elly raised along with Ampai's baby.

145

Sandi, one of forty-six children whom Elly raised.

Amporn, one of Elly's twin daughters, with her children.

146

Chapter 16

A Church Is Built in Phran Kratai

After the burning of Phran Kratai Elly decided to hurry and build a church on the property that she had bought with Mrs. Gulab's contribution. "I was able to buy five *rai*. One *rai* measures 80 meters by 80 meters, approximately 260 feet by 260 feet, so we had a nice piece of land on which to build. Mrs. Gulab is a dear friend and has a very loving spirit toward the Lord's people.

"Also the twins had a golden chain and I had a golden chain and a golden cross, so I decided to sell this gold and use the money to build the church. We put up the walls of teakwood with that. Mr. Gulab gave us twenty thousand baht ($1,000) to finish the church and put the roof on. Brother Cole and others also contributed. Finally we had the church finished in the spring of 1970." It was a large two-story teakwood structure, forty feet by sixty feet. It had a cement floor and was furnished with simple, homemade wooden pews. Elly furnished the second floor for living quarters for her family.

"The church was dedicated on April 5, 1970. Mrs. Gulab attended the dedication, as well as the mayor of Phran Kratai, the chief of police, and other high officials of the town. We had a special dinner for them in the evening."

Five years after Elly was asked to leave the mission with its three buildings, leprosy clinics, and the Land Rover God blessed her with friends, transportation, a congregation, and a church. The transition was awkward, because a little dog that belonged to one of her former associates kept following Elly in the marketplace and the mission mail kept coming to her house in the market. When she tried to take the mail to the missionaries, however, their response was very cold. It was obvious that instead of "hearing the gospel gladly," they felt that their fellow missionary had been deceived by heresy. Later one of the missionaries was involved in an accident with a Thai citizen and had to leave Thailand hurriedly. The work dwindled.

Elly recalled a strange experience that happened while she was still in the mission. Two American girls and a Canadian girl, Agnes Snyder, were staying at the mission. Elly had visitors from Bangkok, one of whom was Brother Chaiyong. "We went to visit the missionary girls. They were nice to us, served us coffee, and talked with us for a while. We closed our visit with prayer. As we were praying, suddenly Agnes began to speak in tongues. As she was speaking, it began to dawn on me that I was seeing her words as if they were written. I understood what she was saying. This was my first experience to understand and interpret a message in other tongues. She said that God was going to pour out a great blessing on the dry land, that we were going to see many people come to the Lord, that the Lord was going to show signs and wonders, and that the church would grow increasingly. As she talked and I interpreted, I began to wonder who was going to get that blessing. There were many missionaries, and I was but one. But today I can truly say that the blessing fell down on the work that God has given me. It has been blessed with signs and wonders and has greatly increased, because it was the church under the name of Jesus."

After this, Agnes and her husband, James, moved to Sukothai, the old capital, for a while. Still later they relocated again.

Meanwhile the government improved its health care services. This relieved Elly from some nursing responsibility, and she was free to do more as a missionary and an evangelist. God blessed the preaching and teaching of His Word. Through her ministry many souls heard the full gospel, were baptized in Jesus' name and received the Holy Ghost.

After the church was built Elly faced still another challenge. How could the church survive without outside support? How could the pastors survive? Elly had no regular support; the church and the workers had to be self-supporting. Although most of the land was farm land, the soil was very poor. Rice was the principal crop in the area.

Elly recalls, "I tried a lot of things. I tried to build up a chicken farm, and that didn't work very well because we had a draught and a very hot spell and the chickens got sick and died. Then I tried growing mushrooms, but that seemed to be seasonal, primarily during the rainy season which is only a few months long. Then we tried to work with wood, because there was jungle all around our place. Phran Kratai is rich with all sorts of wood. But the teakwood is protected by law and can be used only by those who have permission to do so."

Finally Elly obtained a woodworking machine which could be used to make table legs, chairs, and cupboards. Ping soon became very skillful in using this woodworking machine and taught several of the young people in the church to work with it. In this way he could feed himself and purchase the things he needed.

The church work took up so much of Elly's time that it was difficult to run a steady business, but Ping was able to fill orders for table legs when the customers brought him the wood. He also made candelabra for some of the other churches.

"Our first duty, however, was to the gospel, and we often went to different villages bearing the light of the gospel. We had nineteen missions in which we had to do follow-up work all the time. Also Ping was in charge of the youth work in Phran Kratai. Plus there were numerous calls for prayer, marriages, and funerals."

In Phran Kratai if somebody is taken out of this life, the family keeps the body in the house until everyone in the whole family arrives. This can take several days, because transport is slow in the country.

In order to keep the body from deteriorating in such cases, the people give it strong penicillin shots. Then they spray the whole place with fragrant substances, but this does not totally free the place from odor. The whole family has to be there after someone has passed out of this life to make the various decisions that are necessary, and everyone in the church participates, too.

The bereaved family has a rice pot boiling all the time, and they put some fish, some peanuts, and maybe some pork into it. They serve this with salt and vegetables. If they are very poor they may serve just water to drink, but if they are better off, they try to get some kind of fruit juice or coconut water. The church young people come with their musical instruments, including drums, guitars, and Thai musical instruments. They begin to play and sing and testify. There will be teaching and preaching, and almost the whole town will be part of the occasion. This becomes a good opportunity to tell the people about Jesus, about life and death, and about the blessings of serving God. The believers have often been able to reach the hearts of people and turn them to the Lord when a bereaved family comes together.

If there is a dead body in a house no one sleeps. Death is a dreaded presence that robs every activity of meaning. The waiting time may be two nights or it may be three days and two nights. The family members may take turns and rest a bit. When a death occurs, the saints go to comfort, sing, play, and witness for the Lord. They use every opportunity to witness whenever a burial is to take place in any town where there are saints."

Every Saturday Elly conducted a Bible school for anyone who wanted to study the Bible. Many of the young people who were out of school on Saturday came about nine o'clock in the morning and had a Bible lesson. After the class Elly took them to several places for evangelistic services, returning to the church about two or three in the afternoon. Elly enjoyed challenging the young people to study the Word of God and witness. She often asked, "Where do you think we should go next?" Together they planned and journeyed on numerous evangelistic trips.

Elly stands in front of the old teakwood church with her living quarters upstairs.

Thai men enjoy worship and music in the Nong Na Hand church in the northeast.

. . . .

Chapter 17

Romeos and Buffaloes

One Saturday Elly returned from an evangelistic trip
very hot and tired. The young people had been singing,
and Elly had been teaching. When she came back to the
church she went upstairs to her room at the back of the
church. The young people returned to their homes except
the ones who lived in the church, the orphanage children.
They were sitting outside in the front upstairs.

Suddenly Elly heard a commotion outside. "Where
are you going?" a voice demanded.

"I am going to see the ma'am," a man replied.

"You can't go to her," said one of the girls. "She is
in her room."

"Oh, sure I can. I'm going to see her."

Suddenly the man walked into Elly's room. Still
dressed, Elly was sitting on her bed reading her Bible.
She looked up and asked, "Where are you going?"

"I have come to see you."

"Well, you can wait outside."

"Oh, no, I have come to see you here," the man insisted.

"We'd better go downstairs into the church," Elly suggested tentatively.

"No, I have come to marry you."

"You have?" Elly was startled.

"Yes!"

"Well, let us go down into the church and talk about it." Elly wondered, Is he on dope or drunk or mentally sick? She got up praying in Jesus' name, "Give me some help now, Lord."

The man just stood there for a moment, then began to walk toward Elly.

"I just prayed and in Jesus' name got hold of his hair. Then I flung my body on top of his back, got hold of his T-shirt, and turned around until he could get no more air. When he finally turned yellow-green, I got hold of his trousers and his back, pulled him up, and walked him out of my room. I walked him past all the young ones. I told them, 'When I get him down the staircase, you close the stairs here and lock the door, because you might get hurt!' I did a lot of praying as I shoved this man downstairs. 'God, send me some help.' Because I had learned karate during World War II, I was able to hold him in such a way that he was unable to get hold of me.

"When we came down into the church, I heard the noise of the motorbike and I was very thankful. I saw that Brother Plum had come back from evangelistic work."

When Brother Plum walked in he asked, "What's going on here?"

The man answered, "You just don't touch us, or I will

154

put my fist in your face."

Worried about Elly, Brother Plum walked toward the man, who continued to threaten him. When the man's attention was diverted to Brother Plum, Elly got a better hold on him, walked him out onto the grass outside the church, threw him down on the ground, and called out, "Brother Plum, come and help me!" Brother Plum grabbed the man's hands and cried to Elly, "Loose the dog and take its chain! We'll chain him up." Quickly Elly sent one of the girls on the motor bicycle to the police station. A police car came with five officers. They took the man to the station and jailed him.

The next morning Elly went to the station. "Do you want to prosecute, Miss Hansen?"

"No, I don't want to prosecute. You just tell him that he had better not get involved in a matter like that again. I could have hurt him real bad." Whether a problem involved drunks or robbers, when action was required Elly acted. The man was warned severely and released.

The church was built, and God was blessing, but sinners with problems became Christians with problems. Trials were still a part of life.

Visitors came to Phran Kratai now and then. One spring about Easter, some young Chinese men visited the church. "We believe and have been baptized in Jesus' name. Can we have a service?" Elly called for a special service and included foot washing. The Holy Ghost came down, and a prophecy was given to the church: "Have faith; be strong and steadfast in all that you do."

After the foot washing service two boys came with a problem. "Bandits have stolen our buffaloes." Water buffaloes are a very valuable asset in Thailand. Elly called the church to pray, and she and some of her workers went to visit the family to find out more about the robbery. "Let us pray," Elly suggested to the family. As they were kneeling in prayer one of the Chinese men spoke in tongues and Elly interpreted. "The Lord gave me the interpretation that we would find the buffaloes on Bear Mountain."

"That would be dumb of the bandits," objected the wife of the family. "That's not very far from here."

"Well, let us pray again," suggested Elly.

The man again began to speak in the Holy Ghost and again he gave the same message. This time the woman began to cry and said, "The buffaloes are at Bear Mountain."

The family sent someone to the mountain, and when he returned he reported, "There are three buffaloes tied in the bushes on Bear Mountain."

At this confirmation Elly took the family and sixteen workers to Bear Mountain. "A little way from the road beyond three or four rice paddies were the buffaloes. We all took our Bibles in our hands and crossed the rice paddies. Two of our workers got the buffaloes. As they were doing that, shotguns went off a little farther away, but our workers led the buffaloes to the road and walked them back to the owner's home. We kind of danced back over those rice paddies to the sound of gunshots.

"Later a story went around in town that the Christians who went to get the buffaloes were surrounded by soldiers with guns. Whoever these soldiers were, we don't know. The bandits may have seen a vision, for we only brought Bibles in our hands. In any case the man got his buffaloes back by prayer, tongues and interpretation, and acting upon what God said." Christians with problems could call on a prayer-answering God for help.

After this incident the news went out all over town, and many people came to church—bandits, murderers, opium smokers, hashish smokers, and alcoholics. Many of these people were delivered from their sins and addictions.

Elly met many people in everyday life and witnessed on every possible occasion. While she and her workers were digging a well, a neighbor came to talk with her. "Can your God forgive a man who has killed others?" he asked.

"Any confessed sin can be forgiven," Elly replied.

"I had an enemy who tried to kill me time and time again. I did not have a gun. I only had a knife as a weapon. One day we met face to face, and my enemy had two shotguns. He shot at me but he missed. I lunged at him with my long knife, and I chopped him into pieces. Can I be forgiven?" The man repented and was baptized in Jesus' name along with his whole family. He had five children.

In Phran Kratai when a family asked to baptized in Jesus' name Elly first asked, "Do you have any spirit houses—small buildings on your property dedicated to the forces of darkness or enclosed altars in which you offer food and wine to spirits?"

Many Thais do have such spirit houses, but Elly and her workers would pull them down, stand around them in a ring, and put a match to them and to the wooden gods and animal figures they contain. They would ask the new believer to hold the spirit house down while they prayed and pleaded the blood of Jesus, and they would ask them to be the one to put the match to the thing, so that they would never turn back to their old worship. In this way the converts would know they had done this with their own strength, with God helping them.

One man had several spirit houses, and he burned all of them down when he turned to the Lord. He was a strong spirit worshiper and a spirit doctor. He was frequently consulted throughout the town when people became sick. He would go into a trance and claim to have a message from the spirit world. He would tell a person what to pay to be healed by the help of the spirits. He usually asked for a pig, a chicken, a duck, rice, money, eggs, or vegetables, as well as candlesticks and joss sticks (incense sticks burned to spirits for good luck). He usually received a cash payment of three and a half dollars for his services.

The whole neighborhood often got to enjoy the pig. The people were always hungry for meat, so they use any opportunity to get some. If somebody was sick, the people would talk with the spirit doctor. If he was called the whole village is treated to a feast of pig. They killed and served the pig in front of the spirit house. When the food was ready, with the good smell of piping hot meat, the spirit doctor invited the spirit world to the feast. He chanted until he went into a trancelike state. He claimed to commune with the spirit world, and if he concluded that the spirit world is satisfied with the meal, he would promise a healing. Then everybody ate, first the men, then the young boys, and finally the women and children.

It was very expensive for families of sick people. Some of them were ruined when sickness struck their home. Some got a promise of healing that never took place, and they had the added expense of a funeral.

The spirit doctors are often very intelligent, and they always have a way to get out of a matter in a nice and promising way. If their prophecies fail to come true, they just claim that the person has forgotten to do something required, that he has not done something with his whole heart, or that something was not done good enough. Because of that the spirits' feelings were supposedly hurt and they became angry. Oriental people generally believe strongly in this darkness and mystery. They are afraid of the spirit world, and they try to be reverent torwards the spirits. They believe that sickness and accidents are caused by the spirit world. When these things happen they examine themselves: "Why did this happen?" "What did we forget?" "Where did we not please the spirit world?"

The onetime spirit doctor did not continue long in his repented life. He had been able to make a good income from his spirit doctor business. He was tempted by his lack of money, and when his children became sick, he started to go back to his old ways. He began to miss church occasionally. Finally he missed church for a month.

One night about midnight one of his children came yelling and screaming, "Help! Please come to my father's house."

Elly was not sure what to do because several dark, dreadfully dangerous incidents had happened involving spirit worship. Shortly before this, when Brother and Sister Cole, were staying in her room in the church two men were shot down with machine guns just behind the church. So on this occasion Ping called out, "Who is it?"

The child gave his name and pleaded, "My father has been hurt badly, and he wants Sister Elly to come and pray for him."

Elly and some others went over to his house. They found out that the man had been working in the jungle, cutting down trees and loading them on a big truck owned by his nephew. Just as the truck pulled away, someone pushed the man down between the trailer and the truck so that the double wheels of a ten-wheel truck rolled over him. About eight wheels passed over his stomach. His pancreas burst. Elly tried to take his blood pressure but it went down, down, down. His heartbeat grew slower and slower. The believers prayed for him and took him to the hospital in Elly's car, but his injuries were very severe and he did not recover.

Before he died the man told his wife that what happened to him was not an accident, and his wife was very frightened. The believers prayed again that they would have sufficient wisdom to handle this very peculiar matter in a careful way.

Ping, and his brother, and Elly picked up the body, and the man's nephew took his aunt in his car. He promised, "I'll take care of everything. He will be sent out of this world in a nice way. I want him to be cremated, and I'll pay for everything. I will also pay for a seven-day feast."

The Thai people traditionally believe that from the moment a person dies his spirit will float very close to the house and to the body, so they have a special feast for seven days. Between the first and seventh days the household will go to the temple very faithfully every day, bringing special food, sweets, cigarettes, and money to the priests. Sometimes they have another feast on the thirtieth day, and sometimes they may even put it off until the hundredth day after death, according to how the person lived. If the person did not live a good life they will make merry for a hundred days. They have a big feast for family, friends, and acquaintances from morning until late at night. Often drinking and gambling accompanies the feasting.

Occasionally some use this time to take vengeance for an old grievance, and this may result in another death. "Thai people may smile a lot, but they remember, and frequently they try to get even one way or another."

But the gospel of Jesus Christ delivers people from superstitious fears, pagan practices, and sinful attitudes, and through Elly's ministry many Thai people today walk in Christian liberty.

Brother Billy Cole, revered and honored by Elly and Thai Pentecostals.

Chapter 18
. . . .

Toyotas and Cobras

F rom time to time Elly received help and encouragement from Brother and Sister Cole, who came to Thailand
almost every year. They often brought visitors. In March
1972 Brother T. F. Tenney, foreign missions director,
Brother and Sister Stanley W. Chambers, general
superintendent of the United Pentecostal Church, Brother
and Sister Harry Scism, regional field supervisor for Asia,
and Brother and Sister George Shalm, missionaries to
India, met in Brother Boon Mak's church in Bangkok for
services. Later Brother Tenney took the group, including
Elly, out for food and fellowship.

Elly had been in the north of Thailand so long that
a taste of food other than simple Thai food was a real
treat. When the waiter asked her what she wanted she
quickly ordered, "A hot dog! A nice hot dog would be
splendid!"

When her sandwich came, it was an enormous hot dog

with all the trimmings. The whole group laughed, but Elly carefully saved part of it to take back to Phran Kratai. "A treat for the children!" Then she relished every bite of the rest. Next Brother Tenney suggested, "How about some dessert, Sister Elly? Would you like some ice cream?"

"Oh, yes, ice cream would be delightful. I would like a chocolate sundae, please."

When the huge sundae was served, it came with chocolate fudge, swirls of whipped cream, and nuts and was topped off with a cherry. Sister Shalm recalls how much the group enjoyed watching Elly feast on her dessert. "As we all laughed and teased her, she laughed along with us. Then she sighed, 'I guess I can't save any of this splendid sundae for the children.' So she ate every scrumptious bite. This happened when we were on our way to our first regional conference in the Philippines and had stopped in Thailand for a meeting en route." This was the Shalms' introduction to Elly, but their paths were destined to cross again.

Elly also met Brother Robert Mitchell from Houston, Texas, for the first time that year. The Mitchells became close friends with Elly. Brother Fred Hyde and Brother Leo Upton, an elderly but very effective evangelist, came from the Philippines to Thailand for the Thai General Conference in 1973. Six people from a mountain tribe came to the conference. All six were baptized in Jesus' name, and two of them were filled with the Holy Ghost. Brother Hyde was so thrilled with what God had done that he, his wife, and his son, Michael, moved to Bangkok that year and rented an apartment near the YMCA. When Elly visited Bangkok she often stayed with the Hydes.

The Hydes made many trips to Phran Kratai as well as to other towns to minister. His testimony about deliverance from alcohol and his singing and preaching were a big help to the Thai churches.

On one trip up in the mountains about twenty people from the Lisu tribe came to the meetings. "Who will interpret for them? We cannot speak their tribal tongue." In spite of the communication problem the Spirit of the Lord fell during the meeting, especially on a man from Laos. Suddenly he began to speak in perfect English. His message was: "Heaven and earth declare God's glory. Jesus Christ is Lord. Glory to His name!" This miracle deeply impressed Brother Hyde and he never forgot it. Elly found out that by using three different interpreters, including this man, they could get the gospel to the entire group.

In May 1973 the Hydes, Elly, and some other ministers held a youth camp in Udon in the mountains. They were so close to the Laotian border that they could see the campfires of Communists soldiers.

Ping was now the youth leader of all the youth groups in the country, and he had been very busy all through the week. He took several of the young people into town to get transportation by train and bus to their homes. Afterwards he was to bring the young people from Phran Kratai to Bangkok. Elly left for Bangkok with Brother Chaiyong and the Hydes.

When Ping was about 170 kilometers from Bangkok, a boy on a bicycle swerved right in front of his Toyota pickup. If Ping had turned to avoid the boy he would have collided with a big gasoline truck, which would have wrecked the carload of thirteen young people. The boy on the bicycle was thrown off, and his head struck a stone. He was killed instantly. In the Toyota with Ping were Chu, Amporn, Ampai, and other young people. They all began to pray and call on the Lord.

Suddenly a man came and told Ping to go with him. He was the headman of the town and a family member of the boy on the bicycle. "You should just run off. Give me your driver's license, and then come back and help us with the dead body. If not, the police will demand a whole lot of money to settle this matter."

Although he was very frightened Ping replied firmly, "I am a Christian. I cannot do such a thing."

Following the Toyota was another truck driven by Brother Chaiyong's brother, Sagnap. He telephoned Brother Chaiyong and Elly in Bangkok: "Come immediately." Brother Chaiyong telephoned Brother Scism for help and left hastily to take charge of the matter. Elly and the Hydes began to pray. Traffic accidents are always dreadful, but in some countries family members try to take matters into their own hands.

In the meantime the police picked up the Toyota and brought the children to a restaurant since they had been twelve hours on the road. Brother Chaiyong called Elly, "It is the Toyota that has been in the accident. Ping is with the family of the one who has died. It is going to be all right. Just pray!" Brother Chaiyong went to the family and began to talk about Jesus and Christianity. "I am sure that God will be with us," he assured Ping.

Once again Elly's good friend Mrs. Gulab offered to help. After consultation, the matter was resolved peaceably. The Christian principles that Ping had been taught came shining through during this tense time. "I am a

Christian. I cannot run away from responsibility. I must be honest. God will help me." And He did.

Ping finally arrived in Bangkok about one o'clock in the night. No one had gone to sleep, and everyone was still praying for God to help them. Ping was almost in shock. He felt so bad that a soul had been sent out of the world hopelessly. He broke down in tears, but the Hydes, Elly, and Brother Chaiyong tried to comfort him and help him to see that God would not forsake him regardless the situation.

Elly was very pleased that friends from the United Pentecostal Church had also helped. "At this time I don't think that I had the faintest dream of ever being accepted into this organization. I was Danish, and the United States of America was something very far away. But during this time of trouble I found I could depend on these brothers and sisters who hardly knew me." Since the other organization that Elly had been associated with had rejected her when she received a deeper, fuller illumination of biblical truth, Elly had learned to lean on God rather than on an organization. "Here, however, were persons of 'like precious faith' who seemed to be genuinely concerned about me and my people."

The matter of the wreck was barely settled when one of the pastors down south of Hua Hin had to have a blood transfusion. He was in such bad shape that Elly asked the local doctor, "Could we not get him moved down to Bangkok into the big hospital of Seriraj? I know the doctor down there."

After a long talk the doctor finally said, "Well, you can take him. We can't keep life in him anyway. I don't believe that he will live even to get down to Bangkok."

After prayer Elly took the man to the Bangkok hospital and sat with him the whole night to see that nothing further happened to him.

As a result of Ping's accident, and the pastor's illness, Elly says, "I did not sleep for three days and three nights. Everything happened at once. We got him all the way to the hospital, and I walked straight to the head doctor. I acted as though I could not understand one word of what they were saying, and they all thought that I was a silly foreigner who didn't know anything. I just walked through. They asked, 'Where are you going?' and shouted, 'You can't go in there!' I just shook my head and used my hands as though I did not understand them.

"When I finally saw the doctor, he asked me, 'How in the world did you get in here?' He knew me from the leprosy work and was friendly, but it was very hard to get an appointment with him. He was very important, and I didn't have time for red tape so I made my way through, ignoring anybody who tried to stop me. The doctor admitted the pastor and had him X-rayed.

"The man had nine bullets in him! Two of them were very close to his heart and could not be taken out. But the doctor operated and removed seven bullets that were close to his lungs but had not perforated the lungs. One of the bullets stopped only one-half centimeter from the heart. One of his arms was in bad shape. He stayed in the hospital for two weeks, and I nursed him until I had to leave to teach a seminar with Brother Hyde. It was remarkable how God preserved the man's life, but he did not turn out very well, and he is not with our group today. He went down on the matter of women and money." Elly never knew exactly how or why the man had been shot.

Elly cared for her workers in so many ways and was constantly on call to minister, nurse, teach, and counsel. But she also found that on some occasions although the spirit seemed willing, the flesh was weak. Backsliders and failures were a heartache to Elly as they are to all leaders. She agonized over problems, and as all Christians do, she has had her share of difficult trials, but she learned to turn them over to God and to trust Him.

While some failed and disappointed Elly, she was making several true friends. The Hydes, the Coles, and the Munseys kept telling Elly that she had many, many friends in the United States. "Many people came to visit our work in Thailand, including Brother Tenney, the director of foreign missions."

Elly welcomed these visitors and tried in every way to make them comfortable. Her facilities were not modern. There was no hot water. She told one visitor that she had not had a hot bath in thirteen years.

She also cautioned her visitors about snakes, especially cobras. "They don't like concrete, but they can get in almost anywhere." One day she opened the bathroom door to see a large cobra encircling the huge waterpot that held the water that was used for bathing and for flushing the toilet. She ran back upstairs to get a shotgun but then she realized, If I shoot the cobra I will break that expensive clay pot. Instead she just prayed, "God, rebuke that cobra in Jesus' name and send him away." When she went back to check, the cobra was gone.

When the Hydes came back to visit, they heard about the cobra. Brother Hyde recalls how edgy he felt when he dipped water from the clay pot for his bath. "I trusted Sister Elly's prayers, but I sure kept my eyes open for that cobra!''

Wild animals, including elephants, tigers, wild cats, and wild pigs, inhabit the deep jungles of Thailand. Along with bandits and various poisonous snakes, they are ever present threats in the jungle. One day Ping's brother Mong was taking a shortcut through the jungle to another village when he heard a sinister soft pad behind him. Hardly daring to breathe he kept on. The he heard an ominous cough.

"Oh, no, a tiger! Help me, Jesus!" he breathed as he risked a swift glance. The tiger loomed larger than life. Mong dared not try to reach for his gun. Desperately he prayed again. To his amazement and immense relief he thought he heard the rustle of bushes. Had the tiger turned aside off the path? Indeed he had! As did the cobra that Elly had prayed away, the tiger went on his way and did not destroy the child of God. "What a great testimony God has given me," Mong relates, "but now I will stick to the old paths and not take any more shortcuts!"

Brothers Cole, Chaiyong, and Shalm and other American ministers enjoy the Thai General Conference in 1987.

Chapter 19

Sunday School
Seminars

In 1973 Brother Cole and Brother Munsey assisted Elly in coming to the United States for the international convention of the United Pentecostal Church, held in Louisville, Kentucky. Her first service in the United States was with the Frank Munseys in their church in Hammond, Indiana. The Munseys gave her a warm American welcome in Pentecostal style. She made many new friends when she went to Kentucky to the conference. There she applied for and was granted ministerial license with the United Pentecostal Church and an appointment as an assistant missionary to Thailand. She had already held an ordination certificate with the Thai United Pentecostal Church for several years.

From the United States she flew to Denmark to visit her family and then back to Bangkok, where she met with

Brother Chaiyong and shared news of the conference. But Phran Kratai was home, and she was anxious to get back home.

Before long Elly heard the news of more visitors from the U.S. "The general secretary of the United Pentecostal Church, Brother C. M. Becton, his wife, Margie, and their daughter, Rene, are coming, along with the Sunday school director, Brother J. O. Wallace, his wife, Mary, and their children, Joe and Rosemary. They will be in Bangkok in March. We hope you can join us. We will need you to interpret."

When the Wallaces and the Bectons arrived, Rene had taken ill in Madras, India, and they were quite concerned about her. Once again Elly's nursing skills were needed, and she graciously assisted in caring for Rene. In a short while she was feeling quite a bit better, so Elly suggested, "Let's go shopping!" Elly helped Brother Wallace select large, carved wooden elephants typical of Thai handiwork. "Leprosy people carved these fine elephants," she informed him as she helped him choose the best.

During the services she interpreted capably and seemed to be particularly interested in the Sunday school teaching tips. "I especially like to teach with flannelgraph and visual aids. I hope you can come again to Thailand and go up to Phran Kratai. I would like for the church at Phran Kratai to hear this teaching." The Wallaces assured her that they would be happy to go to Phran Kratai. Later Brother Chaiyong entertained them all royally with a bountiful Thai dinner, most of which he had prepared himself.

Elly liked to teach and was an effective teacher, but she also enjoyed training young men in leadership roles.

Leaders and preachers visiting from the United States gave the Thai pastors encouragement and became role models for them.

In March 1975 Sister Vera Kinzie, president of the Ladies Auxiliary of the UPCI, her husband, Brother Fred Kinzie, a member of the Foreign Missions Board, and the Wallaces, including Joe and Rosie, left again on a trip to Asia with Brother Harry Scism.

En route Mary Wallace read in the newspaper an account of Dutch missionary nurses who were missing in the north of Thailand. Later she read that the bones of the missing nurses were found in an abandoned bandit camp. What is this all about? she wondered.

They stopped in Bangkok for services and then left for the all-day drive up to Phran Kratai. About halfway there, they stopped for a delicious dinner at a local restaurant, but Joe was tired of any kind of curry by this time and he confided in Brother Kinzie, "I just wish I had a Big Mac!" Brother Kinzie agreed.

When the Wallaces, the Kinzies, and Brother Scism arrived at the mission they were impressed with the large church Elly had planned and built there in north Thailand. They met the twins, Amporn and Ampai, as well as Ping and many other saints.

Joe had a problem which Elly was able to help solve. He had bought a beautiful *sitar* (Indian musical instrument) in New Delhi, India, and was carrying the fragile instrument home by hand. In an early morning rush to catch an airplane, Brother Wallace bumped into a door with the instrument, punching a large hole in it. When Elly examined the damaged instrument she suggested, "I think my boys can repair it." They skillfully mixed glue and sawdust and carefully plastered over the hole. Some of the quality of the musical sound was lost, but the souvenir instrument made it home safely to St. Louis.

Mary Wallace had a clarinet which had been donated for the Phran Kratai church. In one afternoon Brother Kinzie instructed Ping, and he began to play it that night.

Joe had his own American guitar, and soon he and Ping and the other Thai musicians were playing. Later he played for Brother and Sister Kinzie as they sang in the services. One of their favorite songs was "I'll Say Amen to Jesus."

The Americans were housed in the only motel in Phran Kratai. Elly brought her own bed linens and remarked, "You know, of course, that no one here speaks English, but it is the only motel. All the saints and pastors have crowded out the upstairs of the church. I think you will be more comfortable here."

The services were great. The Wallaces taught Sunday school methods, Joe and Rosemary sang, Sister Kinzie talked about the work of the Ladies Auxiliary, and Brother Kinzie preached a powerful sermon. The Thai musicians outdid themselves with music and singing. But it was lonely that night when the iron gates of the motel shut on the Americans. "No one speaks any English."

The next day dawned hot and humid. After a lovely lunch upstairs in Elly's apartment, the visitors left to rest at the motel.

Mary and Rosemary shared a room across from the Kinzies'. Joe and Brother Wallace shared a room further down the hall. The doors only had a simple hook fastener. This doesn't look too secure, thought Mary. "Let's take off our dresses and lie down for a rest," she suggested, because the room was very hot. It did not even have a fan, much less air conditioning.

They were just beginning to doze when the door suddenly opened and a middle-aged Thai man staggered in grinning.

Mary cried, "What do you mean, coming in here?" The man began to talk in Thai, hit the wall with his hand, and then strike his chest. By this time Mary and Rosemary had grabbed robes and were dashing across the hall yelling, "Sister Kinzie, there's a man in our room!" Brother Kinzie ran down the hall to get Brother Wallace. When Brother Wallace tried to communicate to the man with gestures, he motioned, "Follow me!" He took Brother Wallace and Brother Kinzie to the roof of the building and finally was able to let them know, "This is my motel. I own this building."

Later Brother Wallace returned and explained, "That man is the owner of this motel. That was what he was trying to say, 'I own this building.'"

"Oh," exclaimed Mary. "I thought he might be trying to say, 'Me Tarzan, you Jane!'" They all had a big laugh, but the man had been drinking and their laughs were still a little shaky.

That night they told Elly of the episode. She laughed, too, but she said, "Of course, we are not quite sure how this man got all the money to build that motel. There are so many bandits in this town, one is never sure."

The Kinzies and Brother Scism left Phran Kratai a day early so that the Kinzies could fly to Korea, leaving the Wallaces to drive back to Bangkok in the Toyota to catch an airplane to Hong Kong. During the long drive Mary questioned Elly about her life, and she began to share her rich experiences. "Sister Elly, what a story you have! I would like to write your story." They made plans for Elly to stay with the Wallaces for a week or so when she came to the U.S. for the 1980 general conference.

Sister Elly interprets as Brother J. O. Wallace teaches a Sunday School seminar.

Vera Kinzie, Ladies Auxiliary president for UPCI, speaks as Elly Hansen, Ladies Auxiliary president for the UPC of Thailand, interprets.

Brother Fred Kinzie preaches in Phran Kratai at a Sunday school seminar. Sister Hansen interprets.

The first floor of the old teakwood church in Phran Kratai.

Chapter 20

On Top of the World

In January 1977 Elly and her friends were invited to visit the mountain tribes who had come to the Thai general conference four years before. They sent word, "We have thirteen more ready to be baptized."

About twenty workers, including Elly, set out to the "top of the world." It was an eight-hour trip walking or riding horseback up a trail. There were no roads, just Thai blue mountains stretching as far as the eye could see. Elly walked ahead at first. The long, hard trail went steeply up, then straight down. It was barely wide enough for one person. When Elly ventured to look down she thought, It might be a mile deep drop. I need hind's feet for this place, Lord. After an hour of hard climbing Elly was ready for help. "I must have a horse. I am out of breath." The tribal people supplied a white horse. As the horse looked Elly over she imagined that it said, "Lady, you think you can make this trip?"

"Sure I can, on such a handsome horse. I am going in Jesus' name!" She climbed on the horse and went on. "Forget that you are well past fifty," she scolded herself. When the trail climbed straight up Elly prayed, "Lord, I need an angel to support my back, or I may slide right off this horse." The tribal people had furnished no saddle, and there were no stirrups for her feet. She just grabbed a hank of the horse's hair and hung on.

Behind Elly rode Brother Mankong. Once she heard him whisper, "Bears! Sister Elly, bears!" Beside the trail two bears had found a honey tree, but one just growled as though to say, "Who in the world are these people?"

Always intrigued by nature, Elly tuned in to the magic of the jungle. The mountains are quiet with no people noises, but they do have their own music: birds singing, and piping, water rushing, wind sighing, and thousands of insects chirping. Added to this was the plop, plop of the horses' hooves. Bangkok with its six million people and its terrible traffic troubles seemed half a world away. Suddenly two green snakes challenged the party, but one of the men quickly dispatched them. "It was the end of the road for the snakes but with God's help, we were going to open a new road—a highway of holiness—right up the side of that mountain to some of God's chosen people on the top of the world.

"I see a bee tree," Elly cried. Not willing to pass up the opportunity of a sweet treat, Elly clambered off her horse "in case the bees were smart." The group burned the hive, got a little honey on a stick, and resumed their trip up the mountain. When Elly tried to climb back on her horse, he walked away and she made a nice landing on the ground. Everyone laughed especially the chap who carried the chicken for dinner. In the midst of the merriment he rode off without the chicken.

A little later they stopped at a glistening waterfall for dinner. "Where's the chicken?"

"Oh, no, I left it back at the bee tree!" They ate rice, salt, and red pepper with a cool drink from clear water out of the rock.

After a short rest they were off again. To cross the river one of the Lahu men cut a large tree to use as a bridge. "Just look up, Sister Elly, don't look down. You will lose your balance." The Pentecostals all crossed safely, and they arrived at the home of the gentle Karen tribal people.

"How much further?" Elly asked.

"About two more hours. Well, you should rest a bit in my house," a kind Karen lady invited. She offered cane sugar and water as refreshments, and after about ten minutes of prayer Elly was revived. Her hostess was a Baptist lady from Burma, and Elly took time to explain the way of the Lord more perfectly. Concerned for Elly's welfare, the lady said, "It's too much. You can stay here until they come back."

"I'll come again, but next time I will have a saddle and stirrups for my horse," Elly decided firmly.

On they went, finally arriving at the "top of the world." Shotguns blasted a noisy welcome as some of the tribal people ran to greet them. "What a joy! You came! Oh, hallelujah!" Their greetings were fervent and they shook both hands up and down, up and down, with wide smiles wreathing their faces.

"With beautifully blistered feet we brought the gospel to this remote mountain tribe," Elly wrote. "They received us royally, and when the Word of God was opened to them, they took it in as only starving souls can. Bible teaching went on for hours and hours far into the night. Brother Chaiyong stayed with them until after midnight with only the light of the fire and an oil lamp with a tiny flame to light the night. They sat very still and listened. Even little kids sat still. Babies slept in cloth bags tied to the backs of their mothers. The smoke burned our eyes, and our backs were cold because they were turned away from the fire."

At last Elly, the girls, and the women lay down on one big bamboo pallet on the floor. Tears of joy flowed as Elly rejoiced in private devotion. She had followed Jesus to the "top of the world."

At daybreak the tribe welcomed dawn with songs of praise sung in parts. Soon male and female voices blended in praise to the God of the day and the Lord of the light. Small, smiling women served rice, curry, hot pepper sauce, and tea for breakfast. For the guests the women offered an extra little parcel containing wild chicken eggs and smoked pork. They were poor in material goods but rich in hospitality and spirit—and so eager to give.

After breakfast Elly conducted the first ladies auxiliary meeting. Seventy-five women came, along with the smaller children. The children were so shy and quiet that Elly hardly knew they were there. They sat close to their mothers, and almond-shaped brown eyes stared at the tall, strawberry-blonde Danish woman as she taught. "You need a school house. You can build it," Elly challenged. "Your children need to learn the Thai language." (The tribal people have their own language, but Thai is taught in the schools.) She knew that they were too poor to send their children down to the lowlands where the schools were. The villages had helped two of the bright ones to go to the Chiang Rai church school.

"The young man was several years past twenty, but he was in the sixth grade, and the girl was in the fourth. They were our interpreters. The people are praying that someone will come up and teach them to speak and write Thai. We in the United Pentecostal Church of Thailand will do what we can. Some of our young people go up two at a time for two or three months, not only as school-teachers but also as servants of the Lord."

On Sunday, worship began at daybreak and continued until the sun went down. After another women's meeting Sunday school began, and the men had meetings at the same time in another building. At half past ten they all came together for church. The little bamboo church was packed. Will that bamboo floor hold so many people? Elly wondered. It did. After worship thirteen were baptized in Jesus' name.

"Do you have others who can teach us also?" the tribal people asked as the visitors left.

According to Brother Scism's report in the February 1977 *Pentecostal Herald:* "The gospel was preached; hearts were moved by the power of the gospel; and before they left, *one hundred* were baptized in the name of Jesus."

Afterward Elly did not rest but planned a youth Bible school and a pastors' seminar for the same month of February. "The harvest is white but the laborers are few," she reported. There is much to do. Pray for me so that I can fulfill my duty to God on behalf of those with leprosy, kids with no mother, and those who would otherwise get no medical help, and fulfill my duties as a teacher of the holy Word, a woman pastor, and a leader of God's people here."

Saints in Udon give a royal welcome to Brother and Sister Billy Cole.

A group of Thai Pentecostals in front of a church which was used also as a school.

Chapter 21

One Last Baby

Elly and other ministers and workers traveled to many towns preaching the gospel. In the fall of 1974 they traveled to Camp Soon, which is located on the border of the province of Phitsanuluk and which suffers under pressure from Communists who hide in the mountains. A few years before a family had moved to this place and brought eight persons to be baptized.

Leaving the car at the foot of a mountain, Elly and the workers walked barefoot on a clay path. Sister Samya took a spill. "Her legs did not obey her, so she sat down in the mud," Sister Elly wrote. When they arrived to dedicate the bamboo church, the joy of the Lord took away their tiredness.

Two men and two women were baptized. They all feasted on the Word, and later on they feasted on chicken. "Right in the midst of a dangerous, politically explosive situation God planted a church."

The week before, Elly visited Sukothai province, where there were missions in Tunglyoung and Denst and a church in Hatseo. "The mother-in-law of the pastor had a stroke, but when the saints prayed, the Lord healed her just as He had healed the Apostle Peter's mother-in-law."

In Kamphaeng Phet Province fourteen were baptized and four received the Holy Ghost. But as the showers of blessings fell from heaven so did natural rain. "As soon as the rains cease, we will go east again," Elly planned, ignoring the danger and the distance, driving on and on with the gospel.

The September 1975 issue of the *Pentecostal Herald* carried a picture of the church in Phran Kratai with this caption: "Elly Hansen, a capable, energetic missionary, engineered the erection of this church building. (She lives upstairs.) She is planning for a Bible school in the near future. She was appointed leader of the Ladies Auxiliary of Thailand."

The August 1976 *Herald* carried an account of Elly's trip to the Yahw tribe into some of the mountain areas in the northern part of the country. These people had heard a measure of the truth from trinitarian missionaries.

Sixty Yahw tribesmen, both young and old, came to Phran Kratai for Christmas. Several of the women made the difficult trip with their young strapped to their backs. Elly began to learn the difficult Yahw language with its eight different tones.

Some of the Lisu tribesmen also came down to Phran Kratai. Although they were very shy and some refused to be photographed, about twenty others posed for a picture in front of the church. Two Lisus were baptized in Jesus' name and received the Holy Ghost.

In the September 1976 issue of *The Pentecostal Herald*
T. F. Tenney, wrote an article entitled "Wanted! Men."
Here is an excerpt from that article:

> I can reflect back to one of our mission sta-
> tions, now manned—or I should say "womanned"
> —by one lone woman. On this station, in times
> past, we have had three resident missionary
> families. Now this woman carries on alone because
> no one has answered the call to come to help. A
> visiting pastor recently asked this handmaiden of
> the Lord, "Sister, why haven't you ever married?"
> With one sweep of a finger, she pointed around
> her mission compound and said, "What man could
> live like I have lived for these twenty years?" The
> pastor personally told me, "Brother, that stung!"
> Could it be that God has had a woman there simply
> because no man came forth to meet the challenge?
>
> And then there is a lady, almost unknown, in
> the northern sector of Thailand. She is a foreign
> national from Europe. It's been fourteen years
> since she has had a furlough. There was simply
> no one to take her place—no one to carry on in
> her absence. She has faced the dangers and rigors
> of missionary life alone. Some time ago she was
> awakened in the middle of the night to find a man
> standing in her bedroom, who announced, "I have
> come to make you my wife." Her former training
> with the European underground during World
> War II returned. She jumped from her bed, flipped
> him, and quickly threw him down the outside
> stairs. Superhuman, divine strength was given a
> woman simply because there was a job to be done!

Elly Hansen did not see her role as deserving any special notice. She did not aspire to be the heroine of a missionary novel. "To God be the glory. He is the Head. I just want to be hands and feet."

The October 1976 *Herald* carried another picture of Elly, captioned, "Preaching and teaching the youth of the Lisu and Meo tribes in northern Thailand." This part of Thailand is called the Golden Triangle and is the area where many tribes from the hill country live. Crime, including traffic in drugs and banditry, is fairly common. These problems hindered, but they never stopped Elly, the Coles, Brother Chaiyong, Ping, and the Pentecostal church from carrying the gospel into the uttermost parts of Thailand.

In May 1977 before Elly turned fifty-six in July, she was faced with another challenge—raising another child. She was in her upstairs apartment over the church having dinner with her family and Brother Hyde when they suddenly heard someone downstairs.

"What was that?"

"Sounds like someone in the kitchen!"

"Go down and check it out," Elly told one of the girls.

The girl came back in a moment with a small bundle wrapped in a dirty yellow towel. It was a newborn baby boy! He had a small bottle of water with him, and tied around his wrist was a note saying that he was born May 1 in a hospital in a nearby town.

Elly sent one of the girls to the police and the mayor's office to report what had happened. When she returned she told Elly, "They said, 'Lord, have mercy on him!' They also said that you have taken care of over forty kids already so why can't you take care of this one, too?"

"But I am almost fifty-six. I can't picture myself getting up at night with milk bottles and all that. Then there is all the trouble of teething! No, no, I just don't want to get into raising another newborn."

"Well, you've taken care of us, and we should have mercy on him. He's been thrown away! If you will just agree to keep him, we will do all the work with him," pleaded one of the girls.

"I'll help," another one chimed in. "I can baby-sit and rock him."

"I'll wash his clothes," another added.

"We'll take care of him absolutely, and we will help with everything," they all agreed.

Even Brother Hyde said, "Yes, we should have mercy on this poor little thing."

"Well," Elly relented, "He's not so poor. He's a strong healthy baby but, oh, so dirty!" She began to inspect the baby and plan how to take care of him.

"He was very nervous with any kind of sound, and it took almost a year before he could stand any sort of noise. If anybody made extra noise, he would scream as if he was scared. He would shake, so he must have been put on the floor somewhere with a radio going full blast. His mother may have been a girl of the street going out to find some more money, and he was just left there. Perhaps when she saw no way to manage she just decided to put him in a place where he might find mercy. So we received him in the name of Jesus."

They named the baby Timothy but called him Timmy. His Thai name was Somchai, which means a real boy. Once again Elly found herself preparing bottles, getting up at night, and walking with a fretful, teething baby.

She did the necessary paper work to get him a birth certificate so that he could attend school when he was older. Raised in the church, Timmy soon learned to pray and sing and clap his hands for the Lord.

"Thank you, Jesus, for my family," Elly prayed. "These people are my people. Help me to be all that a mother should be."

As a pastor, nurse, and mother Elly Hansen touched the lives of many Thai young people.

Thai minister in service in Udon.

Chapter 22

Revival Continues

Blessings continued to fall, but Satan is still the "prince and power of the air." In a Partners in Missions (PIM) letter of July 13, 1977, Elly wrote of widespread cholera and other epidemic sickness. Drought covered the land. No rain for seven months resulted in sickness. "We have cared for thirty cases so far—all kinds of malaria— some real bad. Some did not come as they did not understand how sick they were, and so they passed away. Mother Sahmay came, and we were able to stay with her until she died. She called on Jesus, and with a peaceful smile she went, leaving a girl of eleven and a seventeen-year-old boy. The boy was very sick also." Elly not only nursed this boy but also led him to the Lord.

"To know Jesus and the wonderful power in His name makes the difference in every situation. I am so thankful that the Lord sent His people with the true gospel my way and that He also helps me to take this wonderful truth further on."

The Coles arrived in April, and in their evangelistic services in May and June twelve were baptized.

In Namko, a village of about fifty houses seventeen kilometers from Phran Kratai, the whole village turned to Jesus Christ. Elly wrote, "There was no one left to feed the monks. For ten years services had been held in Sister Chan's house. There is only one chair in that place strong enough for me to sit on, a bench. Everybody else must sit on the floor. When someone real special comes (that is, Brother Billy Cole or Brother Hyde) she will borrow a table." The Pentecostals began to build a church with a tin roof and looked forward to dedicating this special place.

Definite danger dogged the trail of the workers who tried to evangelize. One evangelist was bicycling to a village when the police called for all the people to come out of their homes to be searched for grenades and guns. A couple came out with an M-16 and six hand grenades. The police shot them. The evangelist called on the name of the Lord and continued on his way.

In a later letter Elly wrote: "My helpers and I are just back from an evangelistic tour to three provinces in eastern Thailand. We had the Alpha Bible Course, Life of Christ, with us. Book One has been translated into Thai, and the church is studying it through correspondence. I spent many hours translating, and Chu helped with secretarial work.

"Our first stop was Phichit. The pastor had just come out of the hospital. He was low in spirit but was lifted up by our prayers. We believe he was healed of an ulcer. This pastor supports his family by catching snakes and selling them [for food]. He feeds the small snakes to the larger ones until they are large enough to sell.

"Then we traveled over Communist-infested mountains to Phetchabun. Three years ago the pastor, Brother Baew, a former Baptist, came to the truth and was baptized by Brother Chaiyong. His wife received the Holy Ghost when we were with Brother Billy Cole in February. They received us lovingly and gave us their best. We dedicated a new meeting place in Nongpay where mostly Chinese from a trinitarian church attended. They are now studying to understand the Oneness of the Godhead."

In November 1977 Elly attended the Asian regional missionary retreat of the UPC in Hong Kong. It was a most blessed time of fellowship with other missionaries from Asia. Elly rarely left Thailand, so this was especially delightful for her. She returned to Thailand with new strength and new knowledge—eager to get back to the field to implement new ideas and meet new challenges.

Over fifty young people came to the youth week services. Two young girls made a start for the Lord, and eleven young men dedicated their free time to travel with the gospel team.

Brother Paul Cook, the regional field supervisor, came to Bangkok in January. "Sister Hansen was always there to meet me when I came to Thailand. She, along with Brother Chaiyong and the other workers, tried to do all they could to see that I was comfortable." The board members of the Thai United Pentecostal Church all came, and it was a good and profitable time of fellowship under God's blessings.

Not long after Brother Cook's visit, Brother and Sister Billy Cole and Brother and Sister J. C. Cole came to Phran Kratai. One of the oldest boys in the church was to be married. He had lived there about seven years, attended the Bible school, taken seminars, and helped in the gospel team that went out to villages to witness. In accordance with Thai custom, an intermediary came to Elly to let her know that a family in Namko would like Sagan for their son-in-law. After much talk back and forth, Elly and the boy inquired about the price of the dowry. A down payment price was decided and the monthly payment discussed. The boy sold his sewing machine to meet the down payment. The young couple had nothing to say. They just waited. "Their hands were in touch for the first time when the marriage ceremony was conducted."

Elly decided, We have very special guests with us, and we are not going to lose any opportunity to edify and give strength to our saints. Therefore she asked the new bride and groom, with the saints and the visitors who had never been to church, to stand up to praise the Lord. The Holy Spirit fell like spring rain on the saints, including the newly married couple. They stood with tears streaming and experienced the joy of the Lord. Nineteen were baptized in the Holy Ghost, speaking in tongues for the first time.

Afterwards more than four hundred people participated in a marriage feast. Over 100 kilograms of rice, two pigs (124 kilograms), one sack of green peppers, another of dry red peppers, and vegetables were served. The following Easter Sunday eight men and women were baptized in Jesus' name.

The day after the wedding feast Elly and her visitors left for the Thai general conference at Hua Hin, nine hundred kilometers from Phran Kratai. Elly wrote, "I have been on the road more than four thousand kilometers in a very short time, so maybe it is normal to feel tired." She added a postscript: "Pray for youth camp on April 8-17. More than a hundred should be there in Hua Hin."

At Christmas time in 1979 Elly and the church celebrated a most "blessed birthday" party. Brother Chaiyong, Brother and Sister Ferguson, who worked in the American Embassy, and Brother and Sister Bob Rollins were special guests. Brother Rollins was an American soldier from Minnesota stationed in Asia who had married a Thai girl. When he met Brother Chaiyong, he accepted the truth of Jesus name baptism and Brother Chaiyong baptized him. He received the Holy Ghost in Phran Kratai, along with three Thai saints. Four were baptized in Jesus' name in the Ping River.

While the group were worshiping in the Bosaman church the Holy Spirit directed them to go to Chiang Rai quickly. They left at 4:00 in the morning. When they arrived they discovered that a woman lay very sick, unconscious. After prayer, she regained consciousness and was filled with the Holy Ghost. They rejoiced as they baptized the sister in Jesus' name. Five more received the Holy Ghost, and Elly was invited to speak in several schools in Phran Kratai and Nakhon Sawan. "Bring the children's choir and go with me, Sister Ferguson," Elly invited. She did and the children sang beautifully.

Despite trials and tribulations, political upheaval, economic crises, bad weather, and worse roads, Elly always managed to find good news, especially for her newsletters. "I pray, then walk the floor; pray some more, then walk the floor. Finally I start writing my newsletter, but by this time I usually have to answer an emergency call for my nursing skills."

At the seaside camp in Hua Hin, Brother Marvin Cole from Beaumont, Texas, was the speaker. This was the first time that he had met Elly, and he was impressed with her dedication to the work in Thailand. "When you come to the United States on furlough, my wife and I want you to minister in our church," he invited. Fifty were baptized in Jesus' name, and forty-eight received the Holy Ghost. Brother Chaiyong and Sister Elly taught in the morning, and pastors from the provinces preached the evangelistic messages in the evening service, in addition to Brother Cole's messages.

The youth secretary was Brother Chaiyong's son, Chaywan, and he led the singing. Thanongsak, one of the orphanage boys, made a joyful noise unto the Lord on the drums, Brother Boonsie played the electric guitar, and Elly's adopted son, Sandi, also helped with the drums. Talented musicians played many different musical instruments. They sang Bible verses to Thai tunes, danced, and worshiped God with energy and enthusiasm.

When showers of blessings fall, however, the devil tries to put a wet blanket on the service. One of the girls began to shake but not with the power of God. Elly's skilled nurse's eye diagnosed, "That's malaria." She took the girl to the dorm and packed her in blankets, praying all the while. In ten minutes the girl insisted, "I am okay. Now can I go down to the meeting?" She did and soon was rejoicing over her healing.

Just before this meeting Brother Ping was twice blessed. He was ordained into the ministry, and he received a motor bicycle purchased by some of the generous churches in the United States. Several bicycles were purchased for the young people to use as they spread the gospel two by two each Sunday.

As Elly observed the young people she had trained, she began to thank the Lord for them. She declared, "The church in Thailand will be in good hands long after I am gone."

Saints in Namko, near Phran Kratai, worship in spirit and truth.

General board of the United Pentecostal Church of Thailand.

Regional Field Supervisor Paul Cook at the camp in Hua Hin.

Bob Rollins from Minnesota married a beautiful Thai girl while on duty with the military in Viet Nam. He found the Lord in Thailand.

Chapter 23

Wedding by the Sea

The years passed quickly, and Elly's adopted daughters, Amporn and Ampai, were growing up. Amporn, whose name means "beautiful," was the twin who married first. As is the custom in Thailand, one of the church families came to Elly and asked if their boys could marry the twins.

Amporn agreed but not Ampai. Elly was happy for Amporn but concerned about Ampai. Amporn's prospective husband was Jamrat, a nephew of Ping's. He had finished his military training and was ready for a wife. Amporn did not care that much for more schooling; she wanted to get married and have a family. Jamrat was attracted to Amporn and thought she was indeed beautiful. Ampai was not as interested in the proposition to her, however, since six other families wanted her for a daughter-in-law. She could wait for marriage. "I'm young! I'm not ready to settle down."

Amporn and Jamrat surprised everyone by deciding to get married at the youth camp at Hua Hin. This upset Elly at first, but then she decided that perhaps it was for the best. As a leader as well as a mother she was concerned for her daughter, and so she consulted with Brother Chaiyong, Plum, Ping, and Brother Gordon Mallory, who was visiting from the United States. "They are so crazy about each other and want to be together all the time. What do you think?"

"We think you are right," the leaders agreed. There at youth camp by the sea in Hua Hin, Elly had to find a wedding dress for her daughter, Amporn. She had made an engagement dress for Ampai, but Ampai did not get engaged. The dress was in her trunk—a beautiful pink dress that had never been worn. "You can wear that dress, Amporn. That takes care of the dress; now I need cakes, fruit drink, flowers, and flower garlands for the bride and groom. I must also remember to reserve a hotel room in town for the newlyweds.

By this time the whole camp was excited by the idea of a wedding at youth camp. Elly finished her shopping at the local market. Ping's niece dressed the bride-to-be. Tears flowed. Elly was still shaken by her daughter's sudden wedding. Sister Ferguson, an employee at the U.S. embassy in Bangkok, was the matron of honor, and another relative of Ping's was the best man.

As soon as the wedding was over, the young people suddenly began to march around the church singing gospel hymns. They lifted Jamrat upon their shoulders, put a robe around Amporn, and marched around the church twice. They marched out to the Sea of Siam in the darkness of the night, threw Jamrat out about fifteen meters from the land, and held him there. Then they yelled to Amporn, "You want your husband? Come and get him." The young girl had to wade out into the sea and fish out her new husband. The smiling Thai people knew how to celebrate, tease, play, and have fun. It was quite a celebration!

Finally, when everything was over, Elly drove the young couple to town and served a meal for them, along with Brother Chaiyong, Brother Mallory, and others. Amporn fell into her adopted mother's arms and wept. Laughter, love, tears, and trials—Elly tasted them all. She had been a devoted mother to forty-six children.

After Elly returned to Phran Kratai, one day the chief of police came. "I hear that you say your God can heal sick people."

"The Bible says so," Elly agreed.

"Can you heal my wife? She's almost dead."

"No, I cannot, but Jesus can."

"Will you come to my house and pray for my wife? She is very sick. I'm afraid that she is going to die."

When Elly entered the room, she saw a pathetic sight. The woman lay all shriveled up, as yellow as a gourd. Cancer of the liver, in advanced stages, she thought. As she prayed she felt oppressed and heavy. She turned to the husband. "Although I am praying hard, Jesus cannot work. You must have some objects of spirit worship here, and in order for you to have faith in Jesus you must give them up."

With a guilty look the husband pulled out from under the mattress a bear tooth, a bit of bearskin, joss sticks, strings with significant knots tied in them, and idols. Elly knew that the power of demons was real. "I know when

I have to do battle with the spirits. I never touch those spirit objects. I just put my Bible on them and order the owners to destroy the objects."

The husband was amazed and wondered, "How did you know about this?" He carried out Elly's orders to destroy the spirit objects, and God healed the woman of liver cancer. Eight years later she was still well and had borne two children. She and Elly rejoiced and testified to God's healing.

Months passed, but Amporn and Jamrat had no children. Amporn asked her mother, why? Elly comforted her daughter and continued to be concerned. In the meantime Elly had been asked to travel to the United States and attend the general conference here that year. In March Amporn requested of Elly, "Take me to the doctor. I think I am expecting a baby now. Could we not pray that we would get a boy? Let's also pray that God will work it out so that you won't have to go to the United States before I have my baby."

"Amporn, you can pray about this matter, and I'll pray that God will guide everything in accordance with His will. I cannot make a decision alone because I have people in authority over me." Elly wanted to be a proper role model, balancing love and responsibility.

Amporn got the longed-for news from the doctor, and at every church service she requested, "Pray that Mom will stay here until I have my baby."

One day Brother Chaiyong came to see Elly. "We're going to need you to help us in the Bible school for three months. Do you think you could give us your time from the middle of May until after the middle of August?"

"Well," Elly said, "we will ask Brother Scism and

Brother Cook and see what they say." (Harry Scism was director of foreign missions and Paul Cook was regional field supervisor at this time.) When Elly discussed the matter with Brother Cook, he thought it could be arranged. She wrote a letter to Brother Scism asking to be allowed to stay three more months in Thailand to teach in the Bible school. Permission was granted. Amporn was triumphant and Elly, the prospective grandmother, was happy, too.

Amporn's labor started Friday, August 15. On Sunday she was still in great pain. Finally, on Sunday night Amporn cried, "Mom, I can't stand anymore." Elly went down to the market at about eleven o'clock to get the midwife.

When Elly and the midwife examined Amporn, they realized, This could be a complicated matter; we had better get her to the hospital! "By Monday morning we should have this new baby," Elly reassured herself and Amporn.

On Monday night Amporn was worse. She almost went wild with pain. She sat up and prayed and cried. Elly stood by to comfort. She had not been in bed since Friday night, although she had slipped away to attend church Sunday morning. Early Tuesday morning about three o'clock, she thought, My eyes don't work anymore. I have gotten cross-eyed from lack of sleep.

Amporn hugged her and cried, "You mustn't leave me, Mom!"

"Your husband can stay with you and one of the girls is here."

Elly went down to the parking lot and sat in the car. She immediately went to sleep and slept until the sun shone "Good morning!" through the windows. Wearily she opened her eyes, shook herself, and started up the stairs. As she did so she heard a scream. "That's Amporn!" Three more screams came then a faint cry. "That must be the baby!"

Ten minutes later the nurse came out with a big baby boy who weighed over seven pounds. Amporn had only weighed two pounds when she was born. The baby had been born just as the sun came up.

It was a new day for Grandmother Elly too. "Now, I've got to get ready to go to the United States," she announced as she began to pack for another new venture.

Mrs. James Kilgore, wife of the assistant general superintendent of the UPCI, visits Thailand and meets Elly Hansen.

Chapter 24

Elly and the International Church

After Amporn's baby was born Elly was free to go to the United States for the general conference in October 1980 and then to the world conference in Jerusalem. On the way she stopped in Denmark to visit her family.

She reported to World Evangelism Center, the UPC headquarters office in Hazelwood, Missouri. The Wallaces were delighted to have her as a house guest while she was in the St. Louis area. Mary accompanied her to an inner-city church in north St. Louis and a church in the suburban town of O'Fallon. Elly gathered Partners in Missions pledges and preached in the churches, while Mary drove, listened, taped, and took notes.

"Let's don't forget to do those interviews, Sister Elly," Mary reminded her. "You have led such an exciting life. I would like to help you write a book about it."

"Only if it will bring glory to God. I am nothing; He is everything. He is the chief, and I am only hands and feet. He is the King, and I am His servant."

Although reluctant to begin, once she got started Elly was very open. She shared enough material for nine tapes, which furnished most of the notes for this book.

In anticipation of the trip to the world conference of the United Pentecostal Church International Elly purchased a small Hebrew-English dictionary and announced, "I must brush up on my Hebrew." In Jerusalem she was one of the few in the large delegation who was able to communicate with the Israelis in their own language.

As Elly and the Wallaces were en route to Jerusalem, a Jewish survivor of the Holocaust was in an adjoining seat on the airplane. He showed the Wallaces the concentration camp tattoo on his arm. "I was the only member of my family to survive."

Mary shared with him, "You must meet my Danish friend, Elly Hansen. She helped many Jews escape from Denmark into Sweden."

"Oh, yes, the Danes were indeed our friends. She must look up the monument we have built to the Danes in Jerusalem."

While in Jerusalem for the conference, Elly took time to look up the monument dedicated to the Danes for their help in rescuing the Jews during the Holocaust.

After the conference Elly returned to the United States to finish her furlough and continue her deputation. She visited the Marvin Coles in Beaumont. Lois Hornaday (nee Mitchell) drove her to many meetings in Mississippi, Louisiana, and Texas. "No, I do *not* want to drive on American freeways. The traffic is terrible," Elly declared, although she did not seem to mind the traffic problems in Bangkok.

The time that Lois spent with Elly left an indelible impression upon her. She and her husband have since been appointed as Associates in Missions (AIM) workers.

Elly's 1980 furlough was her last trip abroad. The Thai government clamped down on missionary work, proclaiming, "We will not allow any new missionaries, and within thirteen years all missionaries must be out of Thailand." As a result Elly refused to risk losing her visa by leaving the country for any reason. She went back through customs in Thailand, never to leave again.

Duty waited and she gladly took up the familiar burden: visiting the churches, encouraging the saints, teaching in the Bible school, pastoring in Phran Kratai, nursing the sick, and caring for orphans. She dreamed of one more big project, however. "I want to build a large, permanent concrete church in Phran Kratai. The old teakwood church could catch fire. We need a bigger and better building." Would people help? "Of course, they will. Look at what the Dorcas Sisters from Indiana have sent—coffee, cheeses, and clothing. God always provides."

In the spring of 1981 Brother and Sister Billy Cole and Brother and Sister Poling traveled to Thailand and visited all the churches. The Thai Pentecostals revered Brother Billy Cole. "Brother Billy Cole saved my life in the matter of salvation," Elly testified when she was in Beaumont, Texas. He had first brought the message to Brother Boon Mak in the United States. Then he felt a missionary call, moved to Thailand, served as a missionary for two terms, and returned many times thereafter to evangelize, preach, teach, and encourage the Thai church.

"Brother Cole preached and taught the Oneness of God so that we could understand it," Brother Chaiyong said.

When Elly returned from traveling that spring, two young people from the church were waiting to be married. The boy's family belonged to the church but not the girl's. "We want you to marry us, Sister Elly," they asked, and so she drove to Tahmay for the 10:00 a.m. ceremony.

When Elly arrived she found that spirit worshipers had conducted a performance in order to demand that the girl and boy ask help from the powers of darkness. The girl's eyes filled with tears and she declared, "No, I will not bow to the spirits." She was torn between two worlds—the world of darkness where evil reigned and the new world of light and life in Christ Jesus.

What to do? Elly wondered. It was not pleasant, but there was only one thing to do: tell the people about Jesus and His power over the spirits. The spirit doctor finally took her things and left. A little later stones rained down on the roof of the house, but the young couple were married in the name of Jesus, and Elly thanked God for the opportunity to tell a large audience about the good news of salvation.

Elly continued teaching, preaching, nursing, comforting, and challenging the Thai people—her people—to depart from the works of the devil and darkness and look to the light of the Lord Jesus Christ. She was now sixty years old. For almost thirty years she had devoted herself to these people. How much strength and energy did she have left? According to government figures, less than one half of one percent of the Thai people claimed connection with any sort of Christian church, and this motivated Elly to persist. "I must work the works of Him who sent me while it is yet day. The night comes when no man or woman can work."

In a village church twelve miles from Phran Kratai, Nai Aah, a former spirit doctor, burned all the spirit houses on his land and destroyed everything connected with spirit worship. Brother Cole baptized him at the Thai conference. Aah testified of his new life in Christ. "Now all twelve of my children, most of whom are married, want what I have."

In June 1981 in Phran Kratai, ninety-five young people and teachers attended a seminar. Elly used a large drawing of an elephant for an illustration. "God's creation has God-given power. An elephant has power. Only when it dies does it lose its power." God-given power— that was what she had as well as the faith she had exercised from the time she left her father's house as a seventeen-year-old girl. Many pastors, including Brother Chaiyong, attended this seminar.

Brother Boay, a Bible School student from the north who could speak a tribal language, was there. "I want to reach the tribes in the northern mountain country," Elly expressed. "They are so poor and live in such primitive conditions, but the poor hear the gospel gladly. Perhaps Brother Boay will be the means of going into their villages."

At end of June Elly took several believers from Chayapoon to visit three churches. One of her men students wanted to marry a girl in Chayapoon and Elly went to conduct the ceremony. Then the rains came, and the visit lengthened.

"Let's go hunting," someone suggested. When they

did, a hunter got too close to a black bear, and the bear took a swipe at the hunter's arm. "Nurses are needed as well as prayers," Elly mused as she cleansed and bandaged the wounded arm and prayed for her patient.

On July 3, 1981, Ping married the beautiful Bhrani, and Elly had a new "daughter-in-law." Ping is now the pastor of the Phran Kratai church. Their new home is a room in the church. The two-story wooden church in Phran Kratai always had room for more.

On occasion, Elly the teacher became Elly the student. She was filled with insatiable curiosity and liked to learn new things. One of the women of the church gave her a lesson in feeding silkworms—how to boil them and how to obtain the silk. "I would rather grow cotton," Elly commented wryly.

Help came to Elly from several sources. In July 1982 Sheaves for Christ, the UPC youth fund-raising drive provided her with a new Datsun complete with airconditioning. It was fabulous in July in Thailand which is near the equator and hot and humid.

Soon afterward Elly, Ping, Plum, and a Bible student from the Lisu tribe left Phran Kratai loaded down with Bible literature and other things necessary for a long trip into the mountains. They arrived in Nongpay after four and a half hours on the treacherous mountain road. "Buffalo tail for supper," greeted the pastor and his wife.

Over the years many North American ministers and their wives visited Thailand and went to Phran Kratai to visit Elly and the church there. Brother and Sister F. B. Poling of Tallmadge, Ohio, made such a trip in February 1984. Elly had visited their church while on furlough, and they became good friends.

The Polings traveled across the country, preaching in many churches. Toward the end of their stay they spent twelve days in the northern part of Thailand. They visited ten churches in this area, and many received the baptism of the Holy Ghost. Elly helped with the interpretation and did a tremendous job. In Phran Kratai thirty-two came to pray at the altar, and thirty-one of them received the Holy Ghost. In two other churches that she had helped to establish, eighteen people were baptized with the Holy Ghost.

The Polings returned home after thirty-seven days in Thailand. During their stay they attended the Thai conference at the campground, visited eighteen churches, witnessed 214 people receive the Holy Ghost, and saw 27 people baptized in the name of Jesus Christ for the remission of their sins.

Elly was a great help to the Polings and other North Americans who came to minister in Thailand. According to Brother Paul Cook, regional field supervisor, "Sister Elly Hansen played a great supporting role, graciously deferring to others but always wanting to see that we Americans were properly greeted, entertained, and made comfortable. She was conscientious about interpreting."

Following Jesus had led the humble Danish nurse not only to Thailand but also to the United States and Israel and to a position of influence, friendship, and service in the church around the world.

Chapter 25
. . . .

Showers of Blessing in Drought Time

Hot, dry weather caused the harvest to fail again in 1982. "This means we will have more bandits, and we already have too many," Elly commented, but she busied herself with seminars in Phran Kratai and in Hatseo, Sukhothai Province. The Bible students helped win several converts, and seven were baptized in Jesus' name. "Thank God for the American ladies auxiliary, which has helped us with the Bible student work. The Udon church has also been greatly blessed by the Bible students' work."

In the seminar held in Hatseo, six leaders came from a Presbyterian church. On the last day of the seminar they were all baptized in Jesus' name. Ping and Elly visited another town, Lap Lae, with two of the newly baptized men, to witness to their families. They prayed for the sick wife of one and she was healed. Six local trinitarians were baptized in Jesus' name.

When Elly arrived back home in Phran Kratai, a woman from Kamphaeng Phet came crying. "Sister Elly, please pray for my mother."

"What's happened to Granny Gay?" Elly was concerned about her eighty-three-year-old friend.

"She has been unconscious in the hospital at Bang Rakam since Friday."

Elly immediately prayed, and the next morning she went to visit the mother. When she entered the hospital room Granny Gay sat up and asked, "How did you know I was here?"

"Your daughter came asking for prayer about one o'clock yesterday."

The woman's youngest son stared at his mother and said, "Mother, that is the time you regained consciousness again!"

"I had suffered a stroke, but now I am healed and ready to go home," Granny declared.

"Jesus is still a miracle-working God!" Elly rejoiced.

Shortly afterward, Elly called on her miracle-working Lord herself when she suffered a hard fall. Her ankles, hands, and knees became swollen, and a small bone was broken in her left hand. After Plum and Ping prayed she soon felt much better. "Thank God for my long hair. It protected my head when I fell," Elly observed.

In a youth seminar in Phran Kratai, twenty-one were baptized in the Holy Ghost, and fifty were renewed with showers of blessing. Brother Chaiyong, Plum, Ping, and Elly taught there and then went to Chiang Rai, Namjam, and Barn Suan for other youth seminars. Persons from the Lahu and Lisu tribes invited them to come up to the mountains. Elly sent some Bible students up, promising to come herself in January if able. The Bible students returned, rejoicing that nine had been born again in the mountains.

On the way back to Phran Kratai they stopped in Barnkae in Phrae Province to visit a young family from Phran Kratai who lived in the mountains, where they planted oranges. The social visit turned into a Holy Ghost meeting, and five trinitarians received the Holy Ghost.

Although 1982 was almost over, Elly made one more trip to the southeast close to the Cambodian border. In Chanthaburi ten were baptized in Jesus name, and five received the Holy Ghost.

She left on December 19 to get home for Christmas. Every UPC church in Thailand celebrated the birthday of Jesus. Elly always planned a festival for all who wanted to hear about and see the true meaning of Christmas.

Brother Cook recalls that Elly's trips usually included shopping. Her car was usually loaded down with things that Elly bought for her family and the church. "Sister Hansen is a very conservative person and could make a baht go further than anyone. As her regional field supervisor I usually stayed at the YMCA, knowing that Sister Elly would never spend money for a luxurious hotel. She was conservative in all things. When she finished her meetings and her shopping and got in the car for the long ride back north to Phran Kratai, she would relax and turn all the driving over to Ping. Usually he was in a hurry and his foot got heavier and heavier on the accelerator, but Sister Elly never seemed to notice." Traffic in third-world cities can be very "interesting." Everyone seems to have a heavy foot, and no one seems to notice except older Americans. Ironically, Elly still remembered the nerve-racking traffic on American freeways. "I would not attempt to drive there."

On her next trip north to the tribal people, Elly did not need a "handsome" horse. The road wound up the mountain just wide enough for Brother Chaiyong's van. Although she was past sixty, Elly waded through a knee-deep river and up a steep hill to get to the bamboo house. The winter up north is very cold, but the joyous welcome of the tribal people warmed her heart. A UPC Bible student, Wunn, had been sent to teach these people the Thai language. He was conducting a day school for children and a night school for the parents. Elly sang and spoke in Thai, and a tribesman named Jahsang put it into Lahu. Bit by bit, from one language to another, they managed to communicate the gospel. Nine were baptized in Jesus' name, and two received the Holy Ghost.

On the long winding road back down the mountain, as they crossed a homemade bridge, the front wheel of the van went over the edge. "It was not too steep of a cliff, and in less than an hour we had lifted the van back on the bridge and were on our way, thanking God for His love and care!"

The time seemed to fly by! Spring brought no relief from the hot dry weather, but visits from the Coles, Chambers, Kilgores and Kershaws brought showers of blessings to the Thai people. In the youth camp in April, ten were baptized in Jesus' name and received the Holy Ghost. Another youth seminar was held in Chaiyaphun, where ten young people were baptized in Jesus' name.

Elly next went to Bangkok and the Bible school, where two students from Phran Kratai were enrolled.

While Elly and her son, Timmy, were in their third-floor room in Bangkok, the bed and chairs began to move and shake. Timmy was astonished. "What is it, Mama?"

"I think we had better pray and go downstairs. This may be an earthquake." When they got downstairs several were praying. Soon the shaking stopped. The radio later carried a report of the earthquake.

Back home in Phran Kratai, Elly and Ping taught a six-week term of Bible school. Teaching the young and training leaders were always delightful to Elly, but her services were also needed for the aging and the dying. "Some made a beginning toward victory, some were buried in water, and some were buried in the earth." News came concerning Brother Lah from Chiang Rai, who was the first to be baptized there and had stood firm for the truth. One Friday morning he told his wife, "The Lord is coming for me today. I have been up to the throne room. There is *one* throne. Wash me and cut my hair so that I will look good and clean when the Lord comes for me." At six p.m. his spirit left his body. Elly, Plum, and Ping spoke at the funeral. Baptists, Presbyterians, trinitarian Pentecostals, and Buddhists crowded the hillside cemetery to pay their respects to a man who had lived a holy life. Again it was a chance to witness for Him.

Nai Gamon, one of the first to be baptized in Jesus' name by Brother Cole, sent word from Lap Lae in Uttaradit Province that his grandson was very sick. "He cannot walk and his back is swelling." The day after Elly and the saints prayed, the boy got up and walked to school. Over thirty people were baptized in two months in this village, but the believers had no church building. Brother Nuan opened his home for church on Sunday.

217

The lack of church buildings did not stop Elly from pressing on to do more. She housed Bible school students in Phran Kratai for a month to do house-to-house visitation. On Sundays she sent them out two by two to small churches in the provinces of Kamphaeng Phet, Sukhothai, and Uttaradit.

That fall Brother Chaiyong, the superintendent of the Thai UPC, left for the general conference in the United States, but Elly would not consider leaving Thailand because of visa restrictions. In November fifteen men and women were baptized in the name of Jesus, and most of them received the Holy Ghost.

For the third year in a row the rice crop failed in Kamphaeng Phet. When the rains did fall after the long drought, floods destroyed houses and roads and livestock. Some of the people also lost their lives. When winter came, old people and children particularly suffered because of lack of money to buy clothes. When the Dorcas Sisters from Indianapolis heard, they sent material. Elly made warm clothes and distributed parcels to the poor.

Joy filled Elly's home when three new babies arrived. One of them was Esti-Joy, the daughter of Ping and Bhrani—another "grandchild." Elly was grateful for the Sheaves for Christ car when the baby decided to come before its due date.

At the hospital one of the doctors asked Elly, "What are these girls doing? They give birth to normal-sized babies without pain, talking away in words I do not understand?"

Elly questioned one of the mothers and she testified, "I had some fear, so I prayed and kept on praying until

I prayed in the Spirit.'' She had found a new recipe for painless natural childbirth!

Elly had a picture made of Esti-Joy being held by her great-grandfather. "This old grandfather knows about life and could relate some hair-raising tales from the dark side of life. He is a former bandit with a gun ready to use. He was a slave to opium and alcohol, but Jesus came into his life, and now he is safe in the arms of Jesus. He is a miracle because of the truth!''

Man on the right, who was delivered from opium, brings friends.

Brothers Dennis, Cook, and Poling at the Hua Hin camp meeting.

The church at Sukothai. There are two churches and eight missions in the area.

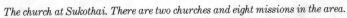

Chapter 26

Evangelistic Outreach

Brother Robert Forbush, missionary to Hong Kong, preached a youth conference in Phran Kratai, and several young boys and girls dedicated their lives to the Lord. A boy from the Lisu tribe whose mother was a trinitarian pastor was rejected and put out of his home when he accepted the biblical truths of the Oneness of God and baptism in Jesus' name. Recalling the rejection that she had suffered as a young girl, Elly told him, "The Phran Kratai church always has room for one more."

Elly kept the Bible school students busy and often sent the Phran Kratai gospel team out every evening. The talented musicians loaded the car down with their instruments and took off. This part of Thailand still had people who farmed by day but who turned into bandits after dark. The team went to two new places—Huylamsay and Nongpay—and prayed about opening a new preaching point in Bongyah.

On Friday at the youth conference a young couple were married, the girl from Borsamsan and the boy from the Kaewdimi church. In accordance with Thai custom, the two sets of parents had chosen the mates for their children and reached an agreement with each other. Elly heard the bridegroom say, "I trust in my father. He will choose the best for me!" Although this is "strange doctrine" for Americans, their divorce rate ranks among the highest in the world. Elly commented, "Let us learn from this. My Father will choose the best for me!"

Thai Pentecostal weddings include worship, singing, and dancing with joy, for Jesus is there. Usually some Buddhists relatives also attend and thus hear the gospel.

After the rains came, the Pentecostals opened four new places for the gospel and baptized twenty-three in Jesus' name. Elly rejoiced in these new opportunities for evangelism. At Lenkatin twenty persons wanted to be baptized in Jesus' name. Elly was especially pleased when a frail, crippled, eighty-two-year-old Bible woman, Revadie, who had worked for thirty years with a trinitarian missionary group, accepted the truth of the Oneness of God and wanted to be baptized in Jesus' name.

Brother Chaiyong came through Elly's province in November on his way north to open a new Lisu church. He stayed for the worship service on Sunday, and Revadi received the Holy Ghost, speaking in a new heavenly language. After service she wanted to be baptized in Jesus' name, so warm water filled Elly's bathtub and Brother Chaiyong baptized her. Also, a young girl who had been suffering from convulsions was healed.

Week by week and little by little the men and boys began to work on a new church building for Phran Kratai.

Many friends from the United States contributed toward this building, particularly Brother Robert Mitchell from Texas and Brother F. B. Poling from Ohio.

Elly diligently translated materials to be used in the Bible schools. She also stayed busy as a nurse, especially when there was a seige of Bangkok flu.

Christmas 1985 was a happy time as Elly planned her usual celebration, using the opportunity to invite many unbelievers to see how Christmas was observed. Most of the saints had to sit on mats on the floor. Six men and women were baptized in Jesus' name, and a man tortured by evil spirits sought and found deliverance. Sinners who were condemned, despised, rejected, and ridiculed rejoiced when the Holy Ghost filled their souls and they could sing, "I Have a New Life." The celebration lasted into January.

Brother and Sister Cole arrived in February, and they and Elly set out to the east to visit churches, beginning in Chaiyaphum Province in a village called Bolahkam. The saints there had built a new church that was ready to be dedicated. Then they traveled to the province of Udon, arriving tired and ready for bed after such a long drive.

The next morning music met them as they came to the church. The smiling Thais outdid themselves to make everyone welcome. Saints and sinners alike came to hear the Word of God.

They left there to go to Sakhon Nakhon and then all the way to Chanthaburi. They dedicated a new church four miles from Cambodia. "A church of wood, bamboo, and straw, but there is pure gold under the straw," Elly wrote on the picture. "Nai Toy gave of his land so that they could have a church."

At the Thai general conference in 1985 the Holy Ghost fell as the regional field supervisor, George Shalm, preached powerfully every night under divine anointing. Brother Billy Cole interpreted.

Two Thais, Khun Lek and Rungrit, began working in Prachin Buri and started Sunday worship in their home. As a result four new churches were started in that province.

Back in Phran Kratai the saints stood in honor of Brother Billy Cole in the new church in Phran Kratai. They were not finished, but they worked hard to make it ready for dedication in early 1986 with the help of Brother Mitchell and Brother Poling.

In 1986 there was no conference, but the leaders planned to visit every United Pentecostal Church and stay for a while in each one. The team from Phran Kratai went to Chaiyaphum and to Prachin Buri near the Cambodian border. They spent a week at each town. Thirteen were baptized in Jesus' name in the new church less than three miles from Cambodia. An old man who was a dreadful drunkard, and seemingly deaf to the gospel was set free after the saints prayed for him. "I never felt so good and so clean as now," he testified after he was baptized.

Four more were baptized in the Wang Nam Jen church. This area had suffered a terrible plague of millions of grasshoppers that ate anything green. Many saints had moved away to other villages, but some enterprising people made a living by toasting the grasshoppers and sweetening them with honey. Nai Nuan, one of the, saints, boasted, "My family made up to sixty batches a day."

On the last day of their visit, the pastor asked Elly to conduct a wedding, "so that we may learn. It is the first wedding in our church." The bride looked beautiful in a pink Thai silk dress.

During September and October, Ping and Elly taught Bible school again in Bangkok. Toward the last of October, Elly drove to Bangkok to welcome Brother and Sister Frank Munsey. "We took them to Phetchabun, east of our province of Kamphaeng Phet. Eleven were baptized in Jesus' name. Then they drove to Phran Kratai, where a seminar was held for young people and church leaders. Ten more were baptized in Jesus' name, and five received the Holy Ghost. Everyone, particularly the talented Thai musicians, enjoyed Sister Munsey's "joyful, blessed music and singing."

December was a busy month. Three new babies were born. Also, three men were taken to be with the Lord. "On Christmas day Brother Chaleam, the pastor of Ubon Province was taken out of this life at the same time that his wife gave birth to a baby girl. Please pray that the Lord will call out some faithful Holy Ghost-filled men. We have but few to harvest this field for God's kingdom."

In all her busyness Elly became sick with a virus that worked similar to Bangkok flu and dengue. She rested in bed from December 19 to 26.

On Christmas Eve a telegram called for help in Hatseo. The pastor's house and his father's house had burned with all their belongings. They only had the clothes they had worn to market where they owned a little shop. Elly took up a love offering for them at the Christmas service. Later she went to help in person. The bereft family sat crying in the ashes as the police tried to investigate. Someone asked, "Why did our God let this happen? Could He not stop that blazing fire?" Elly persuaded the family to come away into a rice field. There she knelt to pray with them and comfort them. She soon forgot her own aches and pains, remembering the night of terror when Phran Kratai had burned.

Cold weather with the temperature down near freezing brought more trouble to the poor. An old man from the Borsaman church died from exposure. Many people have only one thin blanket, and it is hard to keep warm during the cool season.

March brought a five-day seminar for the youth. The Phetchabun and Sakhon Nakhon churches also had youth seminars. The gospel continued to spread, and the church family contnued to grow. In August, Elly reported, "We just baptized thirteen in Jesus' name, and five received the Holy Ghost." Dr. Bhricha, who was running for the new Parliament, visited the church with his brother. At ease with dignitaries or lepers, Elly welcomed them. She had prayed earlier for a cancer-stricken lady from a high-class family. After prayer the lady felt such peace and was so grateful that she brought food for everyone. "She had made up 300 parcels, but we had 350 at the service. We are praying that she will be born again of the water and of the Spirit."

Later Elly's team conducted a five-day revival in the village of Lap Lae in Uttaradit Province, where Nai Lahmoon had built a church on his own land. "Seven received the Holy Ghost and were baptized in Jesus' Name. Khumsyk and Awue, a Lisu tribe boy, both have completed three years of Bible school and are evangelists." Lahmoon, Awue, Khunsyk, and Nai Nuan posed for a picture in front of the brick church. "A house where you can close the door and a bathroom where eyes cannot peek in!" read the caption.

A youth conference in Phran Kratai was well attended, with 125 pastors and helpers present. Eighteen were baptized in Jesus' Name, several were filled with the Holy Ghost, and all were blessed. At a youth conference in Phetchabun five more were baptized in Jesus' Name. Elly rejoiced to see such a bountiful harvest of young people. "They will carry on when we are gone."

After a twelve-hour trip through the mountains, Elly and the workers arrived at Brother Kian's church in Sakhon Nakhon. In the 115 degree heat, sixty-five young people met under a tin roof. Ten confessed that they had been smoking and asked for prayer so that they could stop. A few days later a storm took the entire roof off the church building, but the believers continued their meetings in Brother Kian's home.

As the evangelistic team was driving through a village, a rainstorm brought down the high-power electric lines on a bridge, along with a cement post. Ping saw the trouble in time, and he stopped and warned the others. Many homes were without roofs and many trees had fallen, but their camp had not had a drop of rain! But just ahead of Elly lurked the biggest "storm" of her life.

Elly Hansen's new Sheaves for Christ Datsun.

Brothers R. L. Mitchell, Chaiyong, and Ping visit Sister Hansen.

Asian retreat, November 1986

Chapter 27

Following Jesus
All the Way

For some time Elly had endured a siege of what she thought were hemorrhoids which she treated herself. The condition grew worse, and on September 16, 1986, she entered Siriraj Hospital in Bangkok. The doctor diagnosed her problem as cancer of the colon and recommended immediate surgery. As she lay on the table hooked up to needles, she realized that she was lying there in the form of a cross. She breathed a prayer of submission: "Lord, here I am on this 'cross' with needles in both hands, but You died on an old wooden cross with nails in Your hands so that I might live. I am in Your hands, Lord."

The surgery went well, and the doctor kindly did not charge for his services. As a professional nurse, however, Elly felt that "the workman was worthy of his hire," and she insisted on giving him $200. Her total bill was only

$716. She was in the hospital nineteen days in all and made a good recovery. "I am feeling fine. The Lord willing, I will go the Asian regional missionary retreat at the President Hotel in Bangkok in November." And she did.

In Bangkok she had the opportunity to visit fellow missionaries and fellowship with them. A good delegation of officials from the UPC headquarters in St. Louis attended the meeting. At the retreat Elly felt so good that for the first time in all her years in Thailand she planned to go on all the tours and see all the points of interest that she had never taken time to enjoy.

Brother Marvin Cole preached in the night services and Brother C. M. Becton, general secretary of the UPC, taught during the day. On the first night someone brought Sister Elly to the front for prayer. Brothers Becton, Cole, Scism, and Shalm anointed her with oil and prayed for her. Their faith and her faith soared, and the Lord blessed. The Holy Spirit began to move on Elly's body, and she danced in the Spirit for the first time—a beautiful, floating dance that many of those who were there still remember. Later she confided to the Coles, "Tonight was a special blessing for me. You know the Thai people have their spiritual dance, and I enjoy seeing them blessed, but I have never thought that was for me. Tonight the Holy Spirit moved my body, and it was a most blessed experience."

The Coles selected a piece of beautiful, teal-blue, floral Thai silk and had a seamstress make Elly a lovely dress. She was delighted to wear something different from the practical jumpers with pockets and blouses that she usually wore. She looked lovely in the beautiful dress.

During the free time she strolled through the shopping mall of the hotel with some of the ladies who were attending the retreat. "She always took time to go with us and helped us to select things made in Thailand but, of course, she never bought anything herself," Margie Becton recalls.

"She was very helpful and took me to a shopping center a little way from the hotel," remembers Sister Cole. "There were a number of shops, but Sister Elly carefully guided me to just the right ones. I spotted an interesting looking boutique and inquired, 'How about that one, Sister Elly?' 'Oh, no, that one is absolutely too expensive.'"

After the retreat, a number of the missionaries took a tour to a town on the Burmese border. They had to walk a long way through hundreds of Thai people who were milling around market stalls of food and Thai products. The walk took about twenty-five minutes. When the group finally arrived at the restaurant where they planned to eat a special Thai meal, Brother Jack Leaman asked, "How are you doing, Sister Hansen?"

"I'm fine. In fact, I'm probably doing better than most of you," she added with a twinkle in her eye. Always positive and independent, she did not let her recent colostomy hinder her much. Elly's faith was high. She felt good and was sure that the surgery was successful.

Afterwards, it was time for the long, tiresome trip back north to Phran Kratai. Elly went home rejoicing, full of faith and relaxed after the retreat.

Early the next spring it was time for another general conference at Hua Hin. "Brother and Sister Billy Cole and Brenda and her husband will be at the retreat," Elly heard. Brother Robert Mitchell was announced as another speaker at the conference. Ping and the workers had almost finished the new church, and they planned to have the dedication with the special guests after the conference.

The conference by the sea was a blessed time. Brother Chaiyong and the other Thai people were delighted to see Brenda again. She began to speak Thai fluently after many years, and they had a great time renewing old acquaintance and sharing memories. Elly seemed well. She was so pleased that the Mitchells had remembered to bring her some new shoes. "It's hard to get shoes that fit well here."

Soon the conference was over, and it was time for the long, hard trip back through busy Bangkok and on to Phran Kratai. Elly packed her things and climbed into the car. Ping, who was driving, was delayed a few minutes, and so she sat swinging her leg outside the door. "Put your leg in the car, Sister Elly. We're ready to leave," Ping said as he shut the door.

That was the last thing Elly remembered for the next six days. The group went on to Phran Kratai and prepared for the dedication of the new church. She had achieved her goal and built a brick church in Phran Kratai to the glory of God. The Coles and Brother Mitchell were there, but Elly herself was too weak to attend. Brother Mitchell preached the dedication. Ping and the faithful saints made all the necessary preparations for the big celebration. Visitors and dignitaries were invited.

Although Elly did not remember anything at all of this she did remember feeling very nauseated one day. "I must go to the bathroom. I think I am going to throw up." Somehow she had the presence of mind enough not to lock the door.

Ping was very concerned and noticed when she went

to the bathroom. When she did not return for several minutes, he went to check on her and found her completely unconscious on the floor.

Hastily he put her in the car and left for the long, almost all-day trip to Bangkok. When they arrived at the hospital in Bangkok, the doctors said, "We can do nothing." Ping and Brother Chaiyong were in a quandary not knowing what to do.

"Take her to St. Louis Hospital. I believe they might be able to help her," cried Sister Chaiyong.

When they arrived at the large, modern Catholic hospital in Bangkok, the admissions office demanded 50,000 baht to admit her. Again Ping and Brother Chaiyong were in a quandary. "We cannot possibly raise that much money. What shall we do?" About that time the neurosurgeon, a Chinese who had been trained in Australia and who had examined Elly, spoke up. "I am the doctor. I think I can operate and help this patient. Admit her."

Brother Chaiyong had called the Foreign Missions Division of the United Pentecostal Church, and Brother Shalm, regional field supervisor of Asia, volunteered to fly to Bangkok to be with Elly during the surgery.

Later Elly said, "Had I been conscious I would have never permitted the surgery. I am in God's hands." But she was unconscious, and the matter was out of her hands.

After the long, tedious, delicate brain surgery was over, Elly responded beautifully, although the doctor cautioned, "She will probably be blind and may never walk again." To his amazement, within two days Elly's sight returned and indeed was better than before.

"Before the operation your faces around my bedside

were blurred. Now I can see clearly." She planned to get a new prescription for reading glasses, insisting, "My old glasses are much too strong." She called for a walker and learned to walk again, too.

Immediately after Elly's brain surgery, Brother Shalm asked her, "Sister Hansen, where would you like to go or be?"

"I would like to be with my people," she answered.

"You mean you would like to go to Denmark?"

"No," she answered. "These are my people. I want to stay in Thailand."

Later, during a visit of Brother and Sister Harry Scism, she put her affairs in order and made plans for her ten-year-old son, Timmy, to be cared for by Ping. She told the Scisms, "Whatever God's will is for me, I am ready. If He wants me to go home, then I want to be buried in Phran Kratai. If it is His will for me to live longer, then I will go on furlough."

"This furlough is long overdue," the Scisms said.

Elly continued, "Sometimes God allows us to go through a testing time to see if we love Him as much when it is difficult as when it is easy."

One day the nurses were astounded when they heard her singing. "Why are you singing, Miss Hansen?" they asked.

"You would sing too if you had been blind but now you could see." She left the hospital and returned home to Phran Kratai.

On May 1 Brother and Sister Everett Corcoran arrived in Bangkok to help Brother Chaiyong. Although Elly often drove down to Bangkok to meet foreign visitors, this time she was unable to do so. Brother Chaiyong met them in his van. After a brief visit with Sister Chaiyong and her mother, the Corcorans picked up supplies for a week on the road and started on their journey to the Cambodian border.

On the way they stopped at a village. There a girl from the Phran Kratai church and her husband lived on UPC property and conducted services in their home each Sunday for the few members left in the village. "We miss Sister Hansen," they commented, "but we are glad you came."

Early the next morning the group, passed a Cambodian refugee camp and turned onto a mud jungle road. Several miles into the jungle they stopped at a Thai village of several homes that were built on posts seven or eight feet above the ground. Palms swayed in the breeze. Fruit trees were in bloom, and beyond the village was a field of tapioca plants. A little thatch-roofed church graced the center of the village. Although it was only 9:00 a.m., beautiful singing poured from the church. Twenty-five believers had gathered to worship. "Other saints would have been here but they had to work," explained the leader.

After a blessed service the Corcorans and Brother Chaiyong headed northwest for six hours to Si Thet for a service the next day. About fifty people gathered in the church located about five miles out of town. Then they traveled over the mountains to Chaiyaphum for the night.

Early the next morning they started on their way over rough mountain roads for two hours, arriving about 9:00 a.m. to find around fifty more people gathered for service. Following that service and a time of fellowship, they traveled for eight hours back over the mountains to

Uttaradit for the night, planning to arrive in Phran Kratai the next day.

"They arrived at Elly's house in Phran Kratai about 3:00 p.m. She came outside to greet them before they could get their things out of the car. She was very weak but still independent. She led the way up the stairs to her living quarters. Her house was built the standard height from the ground but the space under the house was enclosed. One section was a garage for her Sheaves for Christ car, and the other side was a large room that housed women who attended special conventions and seminars.

Elly sat and talked with her visitors for a couple of hours but they could tell she was in pain.

While she had been in the hospital, someone whom she loved and trusted had broken open her cabinets and taken money, linens, dishes, and other personal items. This broke her heart. Elly always felt personally responsible when any of the forty-six children that she had raised had problems. Honesty and integrity were her hallmarks. She valued character and tried to transmit her own sense of values to them.

Although Elly was unable to go with Brother Chaiyong and the Corcorans, they drove over jungle roads about six miles from Phran Kratai for a seminar. About thirty-seven were present. Singers and musicians conducted a one-hour song service while waiting for another group to arrive. Finally Brother Corcoran preached without them. A great worship service followed. As the service leader began the closing chorus at 9:30 p.m., a tractor with twenty people in it pulled up.

"We couldn't find any other sort of transportation!"

The singing and preaching started all over. The work to which Elly had committed her life was alive and well. Others were ready to pick up the torch and help Brother Chaiyong in spreading the gospel throughout Thailand.

Among the worshipers was a former opium user who had found deliverance in the church in Phran Kratai. Through his testimony many new converts were added to the church. These hungry new babes in Christ were willing to travel many hours over dark, dangerous jungle roads to reach a place of worship.

The Corcorans left on Saturday for Bangkok. Just before they left, Elly talked with them, "I don't know what God's purpose in all this suffering is. Perhaps He saw that I've had everything going my way for so many years and He wanted to see my reaction when I was going against the stream instead of with it. But I still love him." The Corcorans could see the steady deterioration and the pain that she had endured for several days. Sadness tinged their goodbyes.

On Sunday they were in a great service with a full house at Brother Chaiyong's church in Bangkok. "Our week in Thailand was a wonderful week, with over eighteen hundred kilometers of travel, six services, and eleven hours of seminar teaching. We were weary and yet happy for the great time with God's people, but all were saddened by the steady deterioration of Sister Elly," Lois Corcoran wrote in her diary.

Ping and some of the other saints brought Elly back to Bangkok the next week because her pain had grown steadily worse over the past few days. It was then in both arms, across her shoulders, and spreading into her chest. Once again she was admitted to the St. Louis Hospital in Bangkok, but this time not much could be done.

At this point Brother Harry Scism contacted Mary Wallace, "Sister Wallace, I think you should go to Thailand to see Sister Elly and get material for the rest of her story." The Wallaces hastily made travel plans and left St. Louis, Missouri, for Bangkok, arriving there late Monday night, June 1. On Tuesday morning Brother Chaiyong arrived to take them to the hospital. Mary was shocked to see her friend Elly so sick.

Loyal, loving Thai women, including Elly's daughter, Amporn, and Ping's sister, cared for Elly. The hospital was a large, clean, well-run, modern institution, and Elly's woman doctor seemed very caring and concerned. Elly's throat was marked off with blue for some sort of radiation treatment, and it was somewhat difficult for her to talk. She seemed happy to see the Wallaces and Brother Chaiyong. Mary explained the purpose of her visit, and Elly was glad to tell more of her story of "following Jesus."

On the trip over Mary had organized questions to ask, and Elly was able to answer most of them. Her sense of humor and wit flashed when Mary inquired about the size of the new church and Elly gave the information in meters.

"What is that in feet, Sister Elly, so that our American readers can readily understand?"

"You figure that out, Sister Wallace," Elly shot back with a grin, and they all laughed heartily.

Every morning for a week the interviews continued, with Elly lucid although obviously in pain. She seemed resigned to the illness, and as a nurse she knew the implications of her symptoms. Calmly she explained, "The seed of this illness travels in the blood, and it has traveled to my brain. The outcome will be the same regardless of the treatment."

As Elly related her life story, a consistent theme emerged:

The King comes first!
His work is second.

To Elly Hansen, King Jesus always comes first, and His work in her beloved Thailand comes second. The dedicated, determined girl from Denmark who had decided at seventeen to follow Jesus was ready to follow Him all the way.

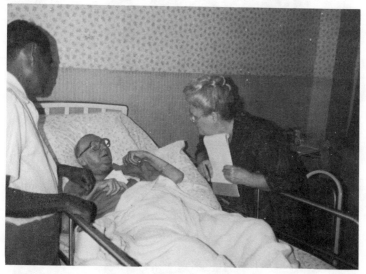

Elly Hansen, Mary Wallace, and Brother Chaiyong at work on her story.

Elly

The new brick church, Elly Hansen's dream.

240